Particolari

Some Treasures of Umbria
and Southern Tuscany

John Yarnold

SUMMERSDALE

Summersdale Publishers Ltd
46 West Street
Chichester
West Sussex
PO19 1RP
UK

www. summersdale. com

Printed and bound in Great Britain.

ISBN 1 84024 218 3

Contents

TODI

CHAPTER 1

ITINERARY 1: Panicale, Paciano, Castiglione del Lago, Cortona, Farneta, Citta della Pieve, Tavernelle and Mongiovino, Montali, Fontignano.

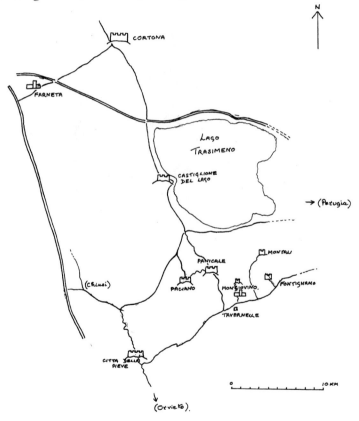

Map 1

PANICALE

Panicale: Piazza Umberto & Collegiata San Michele

We came up to Panicale from Tavernelle: it is probably
more impressive up on its fortress hill above the flat plain
from Castiglione del Lago, a steep climb with the village
always in view. But from Tavernelle, the place grows on
one, after a series of hairpin bends and a steep climb off
the col to a belvedere overlooking Lago Trasimeno, a fine
view so often for us in January and February mists, with
the lake hiding in blue-grey. From the belvedere we walk
towards the old village through a narrow street to an open
space: the gateway, Porta Perugina, gives access to the
walled village with its concentric alleys, but gives little
idea of the beauty inside. At this time of year we are alone
but for locals and walk through to an almost triangular

piazza, sloping upwards to the massive east end of the collegiata San Michele, a piazza made for a pageant performance with a classic fountain on the stage. The one apparent actor is the cure, a busy little man in black who belies his obvious age as he trots down to his car to drive out. We will see him almost everywhere we go in Panicale, talking to his people, in and out of his churches, so busy in his little car. He seemed the symbol of the village, very alive now but, we would like to think, just the same as three or four hundred years ago, without the car of course.

The dominant colour seems to be a dull red ochre rather than grey, as we climb slowly up the apex of the Piazza Umberto and turn to the broken facade of San Michele. Inside it is a great cavern and as dark as if it were subterranean, until we slowly begin to see the baroque shapes of altars, pillars and lofty ceiling. Heavy, dark, and not really the place to appreciate art, it has pictures by Masolino da Panicale, still stubbornly claimed here as a local but who worked more famously away in Florence, and by Caporali, a local artist about a century later. It is almost a relief to come out and walk on and up through narrow alleys to another piazza at the top of the village. This is a most unusual one, recently paved in red, all sloping to a central drain, with high buildings on two sides, a low house towards the view of the lake and in front of us the tower and front of the Palazzo del Podesta, once the great fortress above the village. To complete the oddity of the setting, two ladies with their shopping enter the low house on the right, but backwards into the door and down steps into the house as if entering a boat. The view again is tremendous, over the local hills as well as towards the lake.

Just now we have one more visit to make. Back through the village and the main piazza where the tourist office is closed; the tourist officer tells us so, and where we cannot get tickets to see the Perugino picture, because it is a weekday in January. We made our way past our parked car, up the other end of the modern village. Here is the church of S. Sebastiano, looking not the slightest like a church, but just an ordinary house, with a bell-tower nearby and joined to other houses. But the door is open, our little cure has gone in, as have two old ladies, so we look in and enter while they light candles and show their devotion. Now we are on the Perugino trail which almost becomes an obsession in Umbria. There is his fresco of the Crowning of the Virgin on our left, but it is the fresco above the altar which instantly captivates the attention. The church is light, the fresco is wide open in its expanse to show the shooting of S. Sebastian, the two archers assisted by two others with quivers, all five making an almost calm, statuesque pose, with the hint of a building behind. The landscape of the picture is what must be the artist's view of Lago Trasimeno, in just the blue of the present misty scene from the belvedere outside. No one seems to mind our being here, despite not having a ticket and we eventually retire, sensing a privilege we have just shared as welcome visitors rather than just tourists.

On a number of occasions we took the car round the north side of Panicale, a one-way road where once there was a dry moat for the fortress, to the western gate. Here is another and equally medieval aspect of the town, with a great machiolated tower and the appealing arches of an upper storey loggia. An ancient road or pathway leads up the hill to a magnificent view of the town and a walk illustrated over the three months by a series of wild flowers. A slightly lower and definitely more motor-worthy road took us past a little church, an old monastic farm and a courtyard house, all suggestive of the medieval way to the "twin town" of Paciano.

Panicale from west

PACIANO

Paciano

The upper road from Panicale makes the most attractive approach, retaining the views of Trasimeno and arriving downhill to the top gate of the village. Each time we were on this hill we met various of the ladies of the town going for a constitutional to one of the conveniently placed benches half a mile or so up, often walking in pairs, incessantly chattering. They were very friendly, even if rather surprised to find "tourists" at this time of year.

Paciano has won prizes for the "best kept" in the area and this cleanliness is the chief attribute in a slightly uninteresting place from the point of view of students of art and architecture. Almost all the streets and the central little piazza are paved in bricks, very smooth and seeming to defy any vehicle to use them, while most of the houses have been restored or renovated tidily. Just one palazzo was immense and derelict, that dei Baldeschi, once an important family; even here the workmen have begun what will be a long task. Off the main piazza is a loggia with two very modern "frescoes" expressing the Communist workers' values in field and town, attractively complementing the medieval ethos of the village.

Twice, we walked through Paciano, and although a few figures flitted in and out of doors here and there, the impression was of lifelessness. The three gateways at points north, west and south are all tidy gothic affairs, and it was at these that people seemed to congregate. Next to one of them is a hostelry named and run by a member of the Buitoni pasta family, recommended for food but not appropriate for us at the time. Just outside the northern gate, the main church, smart but unexciting, reminds us of the plague which so often came in late medieval times, with its dedication to the Saints Sebastiano and Rocco. On our visit in January, the cure, of a considerable age, was helping to renew the flowers: clearly, great pride was being taken in the building.

Above the village, on the upper road to Panicale is an old tower, the only remnant of the main fortress of medieval times, now in private ownership. From here we can view the compact village below and then look north to the next great fortification, Castiglione del Lago, by Trasimeno. Even though there is no special art, Paciano represented the Umbrian village at its best, well looked after, with vestiges of history and in the winter months a place of real peace.

CASTIGLIONE DEL LAGO

CASTIGLIONE DEL LAGO

Castiglione del Lago

It is well known that the very familiar and often visited is never really noticed. Was it because we shopped there every week that we only once really visited Castiglione, never went into the big domed church (locked) nor into the picture collection in the main public building? Despite this, the small town made an impression on us, particularly pleasantly while the hordes of summer visitors to the lake were absent. Built on a promontory pointing into the lake, the old walled town really consists of two parallel streets of vaguely old buildings decently modernised leading from a modern square at one end to the castle at the other. While the walk through is pleasant, past among others a very enjoyable restaurant, the route round the outside gave us a better sense of the late medieval setting, fortified up against the lake, whose views were never absent. The occasional pleasure boat and fisherman now seem light years away from the stories of storms on the lake when St. Francis or Renaissance Popes just survived its crossing.

The castle itself, in January and February was officially closed, but the back gate, nearest the centre of the lake, just happened to be open, revealing an irregular courtyard, surrounded by high curtain walls, sloping down towards our point of entry.

Here a stage had been erected, providing a rather special backcloth and auditorium.

Apparently Leonardo da Vinci had at one time investigated the castle because of its special fortifications and one could imagine Leonardo in another part of his many-faceted person putting on a glorious pageant in this setting, with all sorts of "deus ex machina" inventions. The tower up the slope, guarding the approach from land, was an immense version of the typical Trasimeno prow-shaped keep, pointing toward the town. Still of almost full height, dominating the view of the place from a distance, it could well have impressed any military architect. On the north side, attached to the castle, is a curious long wall to the main palazzo building, with a walkway illuminated by small openings all along. Maybe this could be an escape route from palazzo to castle.

Two family names came to our notice in wandering around. The name Caporali appears again here, as well as at nearby Panicale, referring to both artists and poets, here remembered in a church and street, at Panicale by a painting and in a theatre. If only we could give these people real life instead of snippets of information, tantalising and yet encouraging more and more investigation. The chief family in Castiglione del Lago at one time were the Corgna, who also built the crumbling palazzo in Citta della Pieve. They owed their supreme position to marriage into the family of Pope Julius III . As with so many of the powerful families in the area, one of the best-known members was a condottieri, changing sides in the battles of central Italy during the sixteenth century; no wonder everywhere still has the remains of walls and castles. Here, in Castiglione, the great tower of about 130 feet is an impressive memory of one of the most invincible of these forts. Now it could be identified whenever we viewed the lake, often shimmering above and leaving a reflection of itself detached, below in the water.

CORTONA

CORTONA
VIA JANNELLI

CORTONA

15

Cortona

Our approach from the south, just into Tuscany, reveals Cortona stretching right up the slope of the hill, seemingly halfway up a mountain. The road winds up the lower hill past smart villas, through terraced olive groves, up and beyond the crumbling facade of the Chiesa di S. Maria, not visited on this occasion. There were external parts of the town which might be visited on future occasions. Now, leaving the car beside massive Etruscan walls, quite a short walk up via Guelfa took us to the main piazza, crossed by via Roma and via Nazionale together forming the one road on the flat through the old city, lined with good shops. Our future climb up out of the piazza would wait till the quiet of lunchtime.

The Piazza della Republica itself was busy with people overlooked by the great staircase leading up to one half of the Palazzo Comunale, while beside it gaped the archway through which via Roma led down and out of the city. The palazzo, built above and beside this arch, is castellated and of pleasing facade, the tower not in the middle and only some windows balanced, irregularities giving it character. But the real attraction of this piazza is the irregular shape and that it is sloping, even thereby affecting the levels of the lower steps on the staircase. Instead of the planned look of so many centres, this was a real heart of a city, growing up around innumerable meeting moments of time, still living and growing now; slabs were being laid this morning.

Off to the side, behind the Palazzo Comunale, is the Duomo and more especially the picture gallery belonging to it, important for Signorelli and Fra Angelico. A very bored and miserable-looking girl at the ticket desk reluctantly let us pay: certainly no help would be given about the gallery! This was most unusual in our experience; but the contents when reached, were fully up to expectations. We began with a room containing paintings by Signorelli, one of the three artists honoured by Cortona as its sons; some of the paintings were by his pupils or workshop. A good exhibition, of which the Deposition, with a remarkable crucifixion scene at the top background left and a resurrection right, was outstanding, a picture full of real people and many scenes, but so well composed that it never seemed crowded.

In the next room were the two Fra Angelico paintings. The Annunciation, with the angel in distinctive pink robe, was reproduced on card or poster throughout Cortona, and here was given pride of place, mounted as if above an altar. The Polyptych on the side wall, with the Madonna and saints, was obviously less heralded by the experts, but contained in the lower panel predella scenes which were to our taste its most exquisite part. Fra Angelico is documented as being here in Cortona in 1438 and 1439: some books told us he spent ten years in the city but it seems unlikely. The Annunciation is dated about 1430, but for the moment we could find out little else about his visits: so often in our exploration we were coming across stories and settings we wanted to know more about, as well as see, appreciate and where possible sketch. The impulse to research must be one of the most demanding results of these Italian visits.

Other parts of the gallery included a beautifully simple Madonna and Child of Duccio Buoninsegna from Siena, with restrained colouring, the Virgin in dark robes, and one by Pietro Lorenzetti with a dark blue-robed Virgin. The deconsecrated church of Gesu on the site of this gallery, itself had a fine coffered wooden ceiling and retained its wooden panelling. After all this, the Cathedral across the way was relatively uninspired and uninteresting. Almost the most attractive element is the loggia attached to the nave and facing into the Piazza del Duomo, a very simple Renaissance affair. The balcony beside the end of the nave provided views, to be repeated more dramatically higher up the town.

CORTONA
S. CRISTOFORO

CORTONA
S. NICOLO

Cortona: S. Cristoforo & S Nicolo

The next stage of our visit to Cortona was the climb up through the heavily populated streets, no main thoroughfare, but corners and alleyways everywhere, steep and then a little steeper; but none of this prevented the local cars from uninterrupted life. Parked at improbable angles, making their way round blind corners, undeterred by steps: we did not really mind stopping whenever one passed us, because we were being entertained as if by a filmed car-chase. Each moment our previous thought that we had seen the ultimate impossible manoevre was proved totally wrong by the latest vehicle: it was as if the cars, not the drivers, were in charge of the alleys. On the way up, we passed the house identified as the birthplace of Pietro Berrettini, the city's second artist son, known as Pietro di Cortona. Indeed, we could not have missed his name since banners all over the town announced the imminent exhibition of his seventeenth century work. We might return later to see it.

Further up, the cars, the numbers of people and even the houses thinned out. Two beautiful little churches were here, both shut and for the moment we put aside ideas of entering. The sun was shining, the area was peaceful and the mixture of town and countryside inside the walls provided the beauty. S. Cristoforo was a simple Romanesque building, a picture, a setting to be painted or drawn. The second church, S. Nicolo, of the fifteenth century, was given space in books because of the art it contained, but for us the beauty was in the silent courtyard, lined by cypresses with a loggia across its simple facade and an inevitable three-wheel truck parked:

another picture to be made. Just beyond S. Cristoforo was the Porta Montanina with views down the hill to a Renaissance temple, S. Maria Nuova, outside the town and from here looking like a model; across the valley to the hills beyond and further to mountains with a touch of snow; and up, alongside the old walls climbing up to the Rocca and the Basilica of S. Margarita.

We finally left the houses of the upper city quarter, climbing up the Via Crucis, stepped and winding through the trees, and supposed to be lined with Stations of the Cross linked to mosaics by Gino Severini. A new name to us, and the mosaics were nowhere to be seen: but he was Cortona's third artist, of the present century, and we remembered from the picture gallery we visited earlier, the cartoons, lining a set of stairs, which were those belonging to the supposed mosaics, in a post-Cubist style. New names so often appear a second time: is it just that now we notice them, or is there some special law of chance? A few days later the name came to my notice again as I read of his fresco-painting in the Sitwell castle of Montegufoni, as the alternative to Picasso, who had refused the commission.

At the top of Via Crucis was the immense edifice of the nineteenth century rebuild of a medieval church of which only a remnant remained, with a great empty carpark in front, approached by a road from above. We could well imagine the pilgrimage crowds at special festive times, cars now rather than horses and donkeys. This church of S. Margherita was special to the city, more so than the cathedral below, since it was dedicated to and contains the tomb of Margaret of Cortona, local girl and patron saint of the city from medieval times; a widow who especially helped the sick, and founded a hospital in this area. It reminded us that this area, still walled but now almost uninhabited, may in the past have seen a much larger population, although the walled areas in medieval times do seem to have included cultivated rather than just inhabited areas only. The site was a great view point and a place of rest, before we slowly made our way back down through the various and separate stages of Cortona.

We returned to the main piazza by way of a modern hospital frontage apparently hollowed out of old arches and facades, and over the chaos of the renewal of steps curving down into the square. Just before the exit from the city at Porta S. Maria, we found a very special little street, Via Jannelli, almost pure medieval with overhanging upper storeys in a warm ochre stone colour, the final treasure Cortona gave us that day, and another subject for research. Here are the doors or windows for the dead, to be seen in this Via Jannelli, but there seem to be various opinions and much to be learned about their history and use.

S. Angelo, Cortona

Cortona: S. Michele & Santa. Maria

On a second trip to the Cortona area, we visited two sites outside the city walls. The first was the Romanesque church of San Michele Arcangelo on the road into Cortona from the east, at Metelliano. A national monument, sited on what in Britain would be a village green, it is a simple basilica with a west door which was open this Saturday afternoon. Inside, the priest was trimming candles and tidying generally ready for the Sunday mass and he seemed pleased to receive visitors. No Baroque additions had impinged upon the simple Romanesque interior, whose arcades had heavy rectangular pillars alternating with the thinnest of round ones. The almost windowless apse held a simple stone altar. The whole church was primitive Romanesque at its best with no nonsense, and when we came to walk round the outside we found that both north and south doors had decorated blind-arcaded tympana, quite well preserved.

In complete contrast and closer to our original visit, we now climbed the lower slopes outside Cortona, to the Renaissance temple of Santa Maria del Calcinaio. When we arrived there were about ten cars, from various countries, with passengers all of whom were wandering around rather miserably because the church was firmly shut. Suddenly someone noticed that a side door was open; we followed and eventually so did many others. In fact, the flowers and candles were being prepared for the Sunday masses, but no one seemed concerned as we all wandered round this magnificent building. It is the work of a remarkable artist and architect, Francesco di Georgio Martini whose work in both media was well in evidence from Siena to Urbino, as we had seen in both places; he designed this church in 1484. For once the domed exterior was not let down by the interior, which was made especially pleasing by the combination of the grey sandstone of the area standing out in contrast to the cream plastered walls. There was a great sense both of space in the nave, and of height especially under the dome, all enhanced by good light from clear windows. The paintings around were good, if nothing special. We were certainly glad not to have missed this addition to Cortona, especially when on arrival it seemed as though we were fated by bad luck in opening times.

FARNETA

Farneta

On a brilliant sunny morning we came to the Abbazia di Farneta, south of Cortona, just a short visit hoping to see the restored Romanesque church. Entering, we were struck by its stark simplicity, the nave leading up a few steps to what was more like a transept with three small apses, than a true chancel. We knew that Dom Felice had come here in 1937, found an almost unknown church covered in eighteenth century additions, and had spent his life restoring it to its original character of a Romanesque abbey. Surely, he could not still be alive and here, so we wondered who was now responsible for the place which was clearly given much loving care. Apart from a sixteenth century fresco of a Madonna of Loreto, the fittings of the church were in keeping but unremarkable. We noticed steps down, followed them and found a gem of a crypt lit by small windows. It belonged to the ninth or tenth century, with interesting rough stone vaulting and pillars whose fluting and capital decoration spoke of some Roman origin. Written information told us that monks had used building material from a Roman temple apparently dedicated to Bacchus, previously on this site.

As we were emerging from the crypt. the Angelus bell was ringing: an old priest was shuffling about, lit a set of candles and started talking volubly. We realised, though we could hardly make out what he was saying through the peel of bells, that he was calling us to follow him. We did, and for the next three quarters of an hour were whirled through his home, his life, his museum. He was of course, Mons. Sante Felice, surely eighty-five or more, a tiny gnome of a man, calling himself "the last Etruschi", full of bounce, bubbling with the excitement of all he wanted to tell us. First, out of the door from the transept-chancel, we went through his kitchen to a study littered with information about the abbey and the first pieces of his collection. Our Italian was not good, his voice was difficult and yet we were able to understand much of his communication: yes, we must lift this, feel the weight of elephant bone, look at these photographs of different stages of excavating; now along here to the next room; rooms of his museum were unlocked in turn especially for us. True, much of the most valuable material has been moved away to Cortona and to Florence for safety, but innumerable objects were here from his own excavations and restorations, the archaeology and the antiquarian study of the old abbazia. Enthusiasm was exploding, whether with amusement at the fossilised droppings of hyenas, with warnings not to be frightened by the human bones in the next corner of the room, with obvious but totally innocent pride at the pictures of himself beside his reconstructed elephant in the museo at Firenze, or with excited curiosity at the versions of his and the abbey's story in Japanese. He showed us his own cross, a representation derived from his favourite find, a stone mould, belonging to the eighth century, of a Longobard crucifix. It was the sharing of Dom Felice's life's work which was so wonderful rather than the worth of any particular finds. Nothing was too small to be noticed, he never minded repeating what he was saying if we had not really understood, and all the time his eyes were twinkling with real delight, a totally infectious enthusiasm.

When we had been given the full tour, our personal guide said his goodbyes and was off back into his house almost as suddenly as he had erupted into the church three quarters of an hour before. We went back into the church, now again so very silent, to review what we had seen there and now understood so much better. Then we walked round the outside, past the three great apses of the east end. The church was the proud survivor of the ancient abbey, an intimation of the community of the past. No wonder that Dom Sante Felice could be so proud that the full status of abbazia, which it had lost in 1783, has been returned to his church of Farneta, by the monks of Monte Oliveto Maggiore, who had held the abbey from 1500 to 1783.

CITTA DELLA PIEVE

CITTA DELLA PIEVE

Citta della Pieve

To us, Citta was cold bleak and secretive: we never felt
we really got to grips with the place. Our first visit, early
in our time in Umbria, was in January, fine but cold,
making us unwilling to linger in the streets; on our next
visit there was more wind, just as cold and even less
readiness to dawdle. I am sure that on a hot still day, the
brick-built Citta would encourage wandering, but not
in our experience. We had just a glimpse of this late one
day in March when we climbed up the road from the
valley of the Chiana to the west. The sun was low and
the olives on the slopes fronted the red-brick silhouette
of the town glowing in its rays. The result of our
experience is that for us Citta had one very special place,
one area of neglected muddle and a certain point of
frustration.

Looking down on the Val di Chiana, the dominance
of brick gives the town a Tuscan feel, but its associations
are all clearly towards Perugia and Umbria. We were
conscious of being on the Perugino trail and of going to
this Umbrian artist's home town. Parking by the church

of S. Agostino just outside the north gate, the road we took went straight up to the town square. Half-way up this Via Vannucci we were definitely accosted by a little old man, shouting about Perugino. We were looking into a small church, but he urged us next door, into the meeting hall of an order whose robes hung on either side, the hall belonging to Santa Maria dei Bianchi. Our guide was so wonderfully enthusiastic even though I think he was about to close up the room, on a day when hardly a potential visitor was around: he certainly closed up once we left, but never did he hurry us. The far wall of this hall was completely filled with one of Perugino's best paintings, an Adoration of the Kings. The minimal wooden structure over the Holy Family has no reference to the stable of the story, but is all about dignity: the figures in the centre are spaced to enhance this idea. At the same time, to the sides and in the background are many various faces and figures to stimulate interest as we gaze at the picture: the colours are so soft.

Our friend told us as much as he could about it, clearly wanted us to appreciate the treasure he looked after and asked us to write our names in the visitors' book. This was the only time in Italy we were asked to do such. There was a notice: no photography; I had my camera and the custodian, without any idea or suggestion from us, asked if I would take a photograph. The whole atmosphere was so warm and friendly that it enhanced our appreciation of the picture and this remained true when weeks later we went to look at it again, even if our friend was now absent. The appeal of the picture was partly the spacing and composition, partly the familiar local countryside background and partly that here in his home town was this magnificent picture which must have cost a considerable sum, in the oratory for which it was made.

Continuing up Via Vannucci, we arrived at the double piazza centred round the old cathedral. The dominant building is the Palazzo built by the Corgna family, who became more than a leading family of the area when one of them married the niece of Pope Julius III. Since then the family has disappeared and the Palazzo seems to be following them, in the sense that all the fine Renaissance window settings and facade embellishments in soft grey sandstone are disintegrating in a most depressing manner. Better preserved at the other end of the piazza is the supposed house of Perugino's birthplace, but the architecture does not compare. The outside of the cathedral also gives the impression of disintegrating, while inside a dreadfully false impression of marble is produced by poorly painted paper. On the second occasion we visited there had just been a funeral and it would seem a ghastly appropriate place for such. This almost spoiled our appreciation of a number of quite pleasant paintings inside, including two attributed to Perugino which, it seemed to us, were far below the Adoration in quality.

Along the street is the fortress tower, restored, finely machiolated, built in brick, in one part housing an occasionally open tourist infirmation office. The other church, not far from here in Citta della Pieve, S. Pietro, has a supposed Perugino picture, worth seeing if apparently rather damaged. The church was always shut to us and even with help from the office we failed to locate the key, at this time of year. I had already come to the conclusion that I would have to learn more about this artist; first impressions in Panicale and here would lead to further pilgrimage. The views from Citta della Pieve were wonderful: as with so many of the towns and villages above the Val di Chiana, the view from the town's edge over towards Monte Cetona was superbly rewarding especially towards the setting of the sun. The appealing view of Citta from the Perugia road to the south made one forget the cold wind blowing through the town. With a little, probably false, imagination we could feel that the brick towers and walls must be not so far from those left by Perugino as he left to make his fortune as a very successful artist.

Inside Citta della Pieve

TAVERNELLE and MONGIOVINO

Mongiovino sanctuary

The sprawl of Tavernelle does not promise much of interest. Its origin was in providing resting place and refreshment for those visiting the sanctuary of Mongiovino, a Renaissance temple built because of the visions seen by a shepherd girl. When we arrived at the Tempio we were greeted, rather importuned, by a fur-coated custodienne with dreadful teeth who told us many times in no uncertain tones that it was built by Bramante, and who tried to sell us highly-priced mementoes, car keyrings, brooches and the like, out of a sort of garden shed. More attractively, another time, in the afternoon, the custodienne was missing and the building was being used by a group of locals for a service. It is still definitely a site of devoted faith, but nothing directly to do with Bramante.

33

More accurately, it seems that the building should be associated with Rocco da Vincenza, a sculptor and builder of the early sixteenth century, but at least two hundred years elapsed before it was fully finished. The building centred on a dome, has imposing sculpted facades, but the grey sandstone, as so often, is disintegrating and in urgent need of restoration. In fact, first time impressions almost suggest a ruin here, an idea encouraged by the semi-derelict buildings beside the temple. Inside, the decoration is a "little-over-the-top" baroque with some late sixteenth or seventeenth century paintings. It seems that in the later part of the sixteenth century, pilgrimage had developed significantly and many various Italian and Flemish artists were commissioned to produce rich work. The overall impression inside was excellent when associated with devotion but tawdry when linked to the commercialism of the fur-coated lady. Thus, our appreciation of art and architecture may be enhanced or compromised by circumstances of a visit. Beside the main building is a highly decorated brick campanile of uncertain date and apparently in a rather dangerous condition, together with semi-ruinous accommodation once lodging the staff, the canons presumably, who service the Tempio. Now the best impression of the site, and it is good, can be gained from above, on the white road up to the hamlet of Mongiovino Vecchio.

Mongiovino Vecchio

A fortified stronghold on the top of one of the typical hills, it is surrounded by olive groves and with white roads giving access to views all round. Once inhabited by a significant number of people, as so often, it almost fell into ruins, retaining only one or two peasant families. It is now being given a new life by those who can enjoy the remote beauty because they have cars. Mongiovino has defensive walling, a castle tower and an archway fortified next to what was a little church. This is now being developed and restored into a house. On our first visit the track through this archway was filled with a load of logs, obviously recently delivered and being slowly transferred into a downstairs store by one of the old inhabitants. Through the arch, stepping over logs we came on a large house, even a palazzo, clearly restored, with an immediate drop into the woods behind; in front, on the other side of the track, a grass stretch, which could be a tennis court or a tilting yard dependent on your imagination, with its far edge formed of the other fortified wall, or at least its foundations. The old castle tower, polygonal in plan, stands sentinel above. Our first trip, in January on a misty late afternoon gave one ideas of mystery, out of this world, remote and inducing the odd shiver: our second visit, on a sunny weekend, changed this to smiles and openness, inhabitants sitting outside the front door: an inviting place. On both occasions the Dinky toys of children lying around the side of the track gave an incongruous but a very human aspect to a place whose like we were to find time and again in our wanderings around the hill tops and ridges of Umbria.

Mongiovino Vecchio

MONTALI

Montale

One hill along from Mongiovino Vecchio is Montali, presumably having a similar origin, fortified by a rival baron. For us, the visit began by taking a white road which we thought would get us there although no sign post was in sight. The track seemed to go in almost every other direction in turn, wandering up and round and about, presenting us occasionally with a tentative view of what was obviously a castle with a house built inside. We had learned that the house had been rebuilt recently but its exact use was a mystery, lending the trip a sense of wander investigation, to which we would have no final answers.

We finally arrived at a col below the castle where a derelict church, apparently attached at one time to a farm, was the only indication of what had been once a settlement. The relatively flat ground up here would have allowed for a village which would have been self-sufficient in the past, overlooked and guarded by the castle. It is now lost for ever. Along the ridge northwards was a good walking track towards a "holiday on the farm" development: renovation and extension work was going on apace, hopefully ready for summer lettings. Vehicle access was from the north, beyond.

Southwards, but a little higher than the col, was the ruinous walling of the castle, surrounding an area of considerable extent, three or four times the size of the typical Norman bailey. Along one side, very smart new iron gates closed the entrance drive, with beside it a newly restored niche in which was placed a painted terracotta image of the Madonna, della Robbia style, inscribed with a most recent date. Low chains surrounded what could well be a picnic or play area. The drives and borders were newly planted with cypresses and bushes, the main one leading to the new three-storey house, a massive building juxtaposed beside the remnant of a keep wall. It was fascinating to speculate on who might have set this all up, but we had no answers beyond local gossip we picked up. Equally, we had as yet no answers about the fascinating questions of how this all fitted in with the medieval and renaissance history of the local quarrels and life in the outposts of Perugia. The juxtaposition of ancient and modern was symptomatic of the way in which, we noticed, new Italian or other money was being ploughed into old sites, with tourist appreciation and use in mind, in this case, very "up-market". This was brought home to us on our second visit, after a long walk over the ridge to the north, when we met a young Italian couple dressed for the city, she wearing very high-heeled shoes, who had just come from the castle.

FONTIGNANO

Perugino's monument at Fontignano

Having visited Citta della Pieve, become acquainted with many of Perugino's works and identified his birthplace, we were duty bound to find the site of his death, identified for us as Fontignano, a village down below Montali. We soon found that the visit here was not so easy because, although we knew that he was working in the church dell'Annunciata when he died of the plague, we did not know where the church was in this undistinguished village.

On the first occasion we went to the main church, towards sunset, and found the church open and a small mixed choir just finishing a rehearsal. Their leader greeted us, identified that this was not the church in question, rather that the one we wanted was on the way out of the village down there and that we would have to get the key: it would have to be another day. We drove a little around the village, which seemed to have little streets in all directions but no buildings of any particular interest except for a castle up on the hill, above the village but below Montali. This castle was being restored and not to be visited. Of the church dell'Annunciata we found no trace this time.

On the next occasion, some weeks later, one dull morning we parked in the same place by the church and as we got out of the car were met by our same friend as from the previous occasion, the only person in sight in the village. Our friend directed us down to a little cafe, part bar and part shop, where in the smoky atmosphere an old lady very happily rooted out a six inch key and told us where to go. The little church, past which we had driven already without knowing it, was apparently quite old but without any special features, just a chapel. We wondered whether all this really would be worth while.

In fact, when we unlocked a rather stiff door and went into this tiny shrine, we could sense a return into the past, even if there was no recognizable architecture. Sadly, the main work by Perugino is no longer here and we read through the detailed notice stating that this Presepio was now in the National Gallery, London, having been bought in 1895 by W. B. Spencer who was at the time resident in Florence. But there were two other Perugino connections here. A small Madonna and Child fresco is on the wall to the right of the altar, the last work of the painter before his death. The modern art pundits often denigrate the late work of Perugino, and this fresco is damaged and possibly unfinished. But it has a simple gentleness of line we would see again in other late work. Today, maybe this week, we were the lone witnesses.

Further down the church on this same side is a modern memorial to the artist, much simpler than so often is to be found in such a connection, with three simple words Petrus Perusinus Pictor engraved on the side of a stone casket. A black bronze repeats the features of the artist derived from his self-portrait in Perugia, at the top of the memorial. For us, Fontignano, utterly undistinguished as a place, will be a very special memory. It was a good while before we returned the key to the cafe.

CHAPTER 2

ITINERARY 2: Todi, Prodo, Orvieto, Monteleone d'Orvieto, Castel di Fiore, Montegiove, Greppolischietto, Pietrafitta

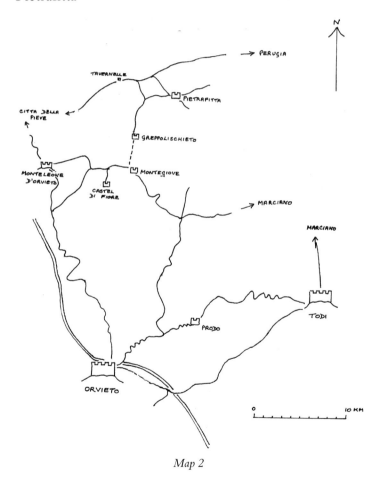

Map 2

TODI

TODI

J

Todi

In January, we arrived at Todi in cold fog, so that we had no view of the town on the hill above the Tevere, but at the same time no hoped-for image that might not live up to expectation. Instead we began almost desperately in dark grey, a misty sky holding down the heavy stonework in alleys and roads, foreboding except that everywhere people were rushing down the alleys across and onto roads which were peppered by accelerating scooters and cars. We had parked at the edge of the outermost walls, one of three successive sets we would find. Through Porta S. Stefano was a feature we were to find often in the following weeks, a stretch of steps with ramps either side for a car to climb, with the emphasis on that last word, climb. We too must climb up Todi by a road variously named Matteotti, Roma and Cavour, illustrative of history but muddling to us. We told each

43

other we would find our way back by looking for the animal hospital we had just passed!

The road, a one-way thoroughfare, down which most drivers obviously raced, led through two more earlier medieval gateways and city walls to reach the upper city. Throughout, the dark grey walls bore in on us, as we went on, up and up, to be released at last to an open piazza, Garibaldi, with great medieval walls on two sides and to the east an open balcony. This name seemed to complete our Italian history lesson. Although the sun was now on us, the view down from the balcony was still missing, just dropping into the mist. This piazza was just an antechamber to the real theatre of Todi, the adjoining Piazza del Populo, entered between the two medieval tower buildings. It was the superb climax to our climb and took our breath away. At the far end was the Cathedral, magnificent in itself, mounted on a great staircase across the whole piazza to the north, providing us with a moment in the slowly strengthening sun in which to view the perfect ensemble of three great medieval palazzi.

No more dark grey. True, there were ochre-coloured buildings on each side, but the almost silver grey of the three great palazzi was dominant, even in winter. At the far end from our stance on the cathedral steps, the Palazzo dei Priori was the most recent, of the fourteenth century, three main lines of windows, surmounted by a crenellated wall and to the left a tower, half as high again, still in a very simple restrained style. The two palazzi on the left were joined together, but more particularly linked by the second great set of steps at Todi, in two parts, first a flight of wide stairs running up beside the Palazzo del Capitano, secondly a narrow continuation turning into the building to a recessed entrance. Even more impressive was the cavern opening, below this great set of steps. The further Palazzo del Podesta was the older part, especially since behind it, now facing into Piazza Garibaldi, was the early thirteenth century Palazzo del Populo. This whole group maintained the theme of solidity, relieved on our view by beautiful window architecture halfway up the wall, sets of openings surmounted by carved stone arches and triangles. On the ground level the walls are all pierced by cavernous arches, leading inside to depths which could be imagined to extend for ever even if we knew there were mundane offices from which so many emerged to go for their lunchtime break.

TODI
DUOMO

Cathedral inside

The rest of Todi was in a sense an extra, almost an afterthought: there was a long list of places to visit which we never really tried to complete. We found some highlights, but all the time our thoughts returned to the Piazza: Todi would always remain for us as the Piazza whatever else we might find. We turned on our steps to find the cathedral facade, true to the character of the great Piazza, but seeming unfinished, with a tower only on the right side of the facade while the wall above the rose window abruptly ended in a straight line. The carving around the central one of three doorways and around the rose window was fine, simple with a touch of pink marble to grace the silver-grey which it shared with the palazzi. Inside, the duomo was a long basilica with slender pillars surmounted by Corinthian capitals and a high clerestory, but in carvings or paintings it held for us nothing that stopped one from longing to go outside and view the piazza again.

San Fortunato

A walk through the streets southwards brought us to San Fortunato which gave us frustration caused by the Italian siesta: we had not yet learned to come to terms with this. The front of the church was again preceded by a set of steps, but this time interspersed with hedged gardens halfway up calming the severity of the city stones. To the left is a statue put up to commemorate Jacoponi di Todi, whom we were to come across again, clearly honoured now as the author of the medieval carol, Stabat Mater, even if the poet was a bit too intense in his life even for medieval Franciscans. The facade of San Fortunato had the customary three doorways simply but beautifully carved, but above was the curiously typical unfinished walling so often to be found and giving rise to various explanations: successively rough lines horizontally, waiting to be finished in ashlar or marble, but still remaining broken and craggy: someone had run out of money. Now the frustration. It was open, it was bright

Gothic architecture and there was the beautiful if damaged fresco by Masolino di Panicale. Was he from our local village of Panicale or a Florentine from another Tuscan village of the same name as experts outside Umbria insist? But whatever, within minutes, the custodian was on us and out we must scurry as he locked up for lunch: we just had a peep, and a memory, blighted by a black cassock.

Our visit to Todi was now completed by a peaceful walk round the Rocca, devoid of its ancient building but giving vistas from view points to the west now that the winter sun had made some progress to conquer the mists of the river valley. On our return to the car, a sign to the Roman forum niches diverted us slightly from Corso Cavour. Here we were returning to the dark grey world as alongside an open space, used as a carpark, was a mountainous wall topped by ancient houses, retaining three great Roman arches recessed, possibly the remains of a basilica, not really connected to any recognizable forum but forcefully reminding us that Todi had been a hillside inhabited and fortified for hundreds of years before it was completed by its wonderful medieval treasures. Everything since seemed a temporary gloss.

There was still the church of Santa Maria della Consolazione, at the bottom of the hill, already seen emerging out of the mist as we looked from above when we walked round the Rocca. A Renaissance addition probably built to the designs of Antonio da Sangallo, it seemed so different from medieval Todi.

S. Maria della Consolazione

We were to find that such temples were often added outside the Umbrian cities, architecture that seemed almost alien in this part of the country despite being so very Italian. Leaving the car again, in a completely deserted park, we could view its complete set of Renaissance facades, built in light golden stone, each one the same except for one missing doorway indicating the internal presence of the altar. All three doors were closed and we quietly accepted that we would not be able to see inside. But a little old lady in black appeared and opened up the Tempio. Inside we found a scene correctly described by guidebooks as over-decorated by huge pedestrian statues and a highly ornate altarpiece. In the middle, today, was a coffin on a bier, together with approriate flowers and candles: the old lady duly lit the candles before she sat down at her stall of cards and votive offerings. Not a word or gesture, we almost expected her to start knitting. This Tempio was a mausoleum rather than a holy place of communal worship, and as we stood again outside admiring the architecture, it was just right that members of a family should arrive, exchange greetings and go to pay their last respects.

This completed our glimpse of the life of Todi in January: speeding commuters returning home at lunchtime and inscrutable custodians. Presumably, the time of year had given us a rather, and uncharacteristic, blank experience. As we left, along the road beside the Tiber to the north, we could look up in afternoon sun to the city of Todi, with its Etruscan, Roman and medieval layers, walls and towers, holding almost in secret the treasure of a well-nigh perfect piazza. To revive memories of our January trip, we returned in April seeing the whole setting from the hills to the north, almost as if viewing a model, and then approaching across the old bridge over the Tiber at Ponteculi, still guarded by its ancient fortifications.

Montesanto, Todi

This approach allowed us to try a visit to the convent of Montesanto, on the slopes below the walls of the city, occupying an almost separate knoll and now a fully functional Franciscan centre. Driving up the road to the convent, which doubled up as entrance and Way of the Cross with modern shrines, we found the esplanade in front of the church facade vacant except for one friar wandering up and down, every now and again kicking a little bit of rubbish, a plastic cup. We asked if we could look in and were told in monosyllables, yes and up through that passage. We went and found ourselves in a beautifully kept cloister, with monks' rooms and offices leading off it, while on the floor above were various meeting rooms with ultra-modern audio-visual facilities, most of the doors to these rooms being open to view. There was also a door, clearly to the church and firmly shut and locked.

We went outside again and found the friar who had been joined by a companion, both idling away as before, and we were told that we could go into the church if one of them went and got the key. Obviously we should not rush them, but when we eventually entered the church we found a place of worship well-prepared for visitors with cards and booklets. Although the friar remained almost silent, he clearly was glad to find we were appreciating his beautiful church. The highlight was a Florentine fresco probably from the workshop of Ghirlandaio, of the Nativity with attendant saints, expressed with a good sense of space and a feel of reverence. There were other pictures including a magnificent Baroque altar-piece decorated by Cesare

Sermei, but unfortunately the convent has lost its masterpiece by Spagna, a coronation of the Madonna, to the Todi pinacoteca. We were reminded that one of the joys in much of Umbria is that so much of its religious art is still in its church setting. Despite the apparent reluctance to welcome us at first, we were glad to be able to leave Montesanto with a good feeling and smiles all round. The balcony of the esplanade in front of the convent then gave us a wonderful view of the whole of Todi, possibly the best one from any direction.

Todi from north-west

PRODO

Prodo

Prodo was an unexpected stopping-place on an Easter drive around the hills between Orvieto and Todi. In the middle of nowhere is a castle with a hamlet attached. Originally the castle seems to have been built high on the rocks above the present village, but was relocated on a more accessible and larger site overlooking a deep ravine. The buildings are restored and in private ownership, imposing towers built around courtyards, with a ramp which was presumably added into the main court at the time of carriages, and terraces below the castle walls overlooking the ravine now in part turned into stabling for a horse or two. One more castle among so many, inaccessible to us: but it provided us with an idea of such buildings in eighteenth century use, with an elegance in an area that surely would have been remote and backward.

The hamlet or village was arranged, most unusually for this part of Italy, on either side of a very wide street, leading on the flat straight to the castle entrance. On this Easter Monday, the street was deserted except for two or three parked cars and two cardboard boxes chasing each other around in the wind. It could have become the setting for a remake of High Noon: we could almost hear the theme tune as the cardboard made its way towards the archway, a variation on a "spaghetti western" medieval cartoon style. In fact, it was just the scene for seven Italians to return to their cars after a morning's hike, and the spell was broken. The place had given a unique moment to our Umbrian encounters.

ORVIETO

ORVIETO

General view of Orvieto

A long, tortuous, up and down journey led us to Orvieto, a Saturday morning journey which could not be hurried but whose delays would undoubtedly make us late for the siesta closures and prevent or compromise our viewing of the expected marvels of Signorelli. As it was, we just got into the cathedral for a short visit, by totally ignoring the western facade for a moment, and then, after a wander round the city whose other parts were so often denigrated by guidebooks but which were in fact interesting and attractive, a second visit to the cathedral. This was actually a good way to do it, and we came to understand Orvieto much better as we gradually lost the crowds of winter Saturday Italian tourists.

From some distance the old city loomed in the mist, a dark trapezoid lump erupting from the valley. We parked below the great mass of volcanic rock, wondering how long the cliffs could be shored up below the Rocca. We hurried through the station to the funiculare, to an experience unique in Umbria, a sort of popping up the cliff in a crowded bubble out of which to emerge in a sunlit bus terminus beside the Rocca gateway. The cathedral, our destination, towers over the buildings of the city, and as we made our way beside the modern military barracks and young soldiers meeting visiting family, we were continually frustrated by an impasse: we had to go left or right and never towards the cathedral. Which alleyway would lead us? This part of the town was not an inspiration and even when we arrived, part of the east end of the cathedral was under the inevitable scaffolding, which also cut off the apse internally.

Inside, the Cathedral seemed at first a poor relation of the one in Siena, the same alternating stripes, especially on the tall columns, with alabaster-filled windows giving a subjugation of light contrary to our Northern expectations for a cathedral. It was crowded even now with tourists, and guides lecturing: what would it be like in summer? On the northern wall of the nave, almost ignored by the crowds, was a fresco which muddled us for a time since it seemed only half of what we had expected from pictures. In reality, the Madonna and Child by Gentile da Fabriano of 1425 had been given a later addition of a Saint Catherine, but both that and the border are thankfully now removed, leaving a very gentle and moving Madonna and Child isolate on the wall.

On this first part of our visit, we spent the rest of the time in the chapel of the Madonna di San Brizio; but to do this we needed tickets, not obtainable on site. Hot foot to the tourist office opposite the west door and a frustrating wait while the only person on duty had long conversations on the phone and with friends. At last, we would have just enough time to see the chapel properly. This is a completely frescoed chapel, or transept of the cathedral, essentially picturing the Last Judgment, painted by Luca Signorelli. A little of it dates back to Fra Angelico, on the vaults, but this is just a technical detail. Luckily the frescoes had all been restored and only returned for viewing recently. Here we really did see the Signorelli, met earlier at his home town of Cortona and who had almost "out-Michelangeloed" Michelangelo with his nudes, rippling muscles, backsides and chests, legs in all contortions. It was extraordinary that such crowded pictures, so full of the saved or the damned, angels or demons, never seemed crowded, except possibly for the main Hell scene, which was meant to be full, I suppose. Various of those represented refer to historical characters such as Virgil, Dante and Columbus; the two standing at the side, Fra Angelico and Signorelli in self-portrait in front of him, seemed to be looking at the whole episode of judgment with a quiet, almost sardonic detachment. But time was limited, very soon we were herded out both from chapel and cathedral by anxious guardians who wanted to lock up.

inside & outside of the Cathedral

Our second and later visit to the Cathedral found very few tourists inside and therefor the atmosphere of the great striped hall stopped being such a voyeurist trap and became more of a meaningful cathedral; even better, the sun now shone through the western rose window. Since the apse was closed, the northern transept chapel became the main focus of our attention now, with the highly venerated Holy Corporal of the story dating from 1263 or 1264 which really caused the great cathedral to be built. Should we believe in the miracle? We certainly wondered at the beautiful reliquary in gold and silver with blue glazed pictures, the tabernacle for the Corporal and the colourful frescoes covering all walls and vault: these together produce a holy place of beauty. To this is added, at the entrance, a large picture by Lippo Memmi of the Madonna dei Misericordia. We were only just becoming really aware of the iconography of this idea of the Virgin Protectress, an image we found again and again all over the region. In this case, the representation was an especially good and memorable one, for its size, the red of the Madonna's dress and especially the serenity of her face. After a long look, we moved on. Despite the scaffolding of the apse, there were other things to appreciate, such as a marble carving of the Pieta, made out of one piece of marble including Joseph of Arimathea standing by as well as the ladder used to climb the cross, the work of Ippolito Scalza in the late sixteenth century. For once, this later work was agreeable to our personal taste.

West door of the Cathedral

The outside of the cathedral, the western front, must be one of the best-known and most pictured in all Italy. The reality in no way belies the expectation of its beauty, and even the relatively recent mosaics or the controversial modern sculpted doors are neither out of place, while the sculpture of Lorenzo Martini and all his many associates invite long inspection and total wonder: binoculars would be useful. The winter sun was warm and allowed us to stand and stare, while after midday the crowds disappeared. Many of the scenes are easy to understand; some, such as the creation of Eve or the killing of Abel, have powerful imagery, and all are now in unexpectedly good, if restored, condition. The figures of the Virgin and Child above the central door and the four bronze respresentations of the Evangelists' symbols on the same level, are clearly outstanding. But the main problem is how far it is possible to take in both the details and the whole facade at the same time.

Between the two visits to the Cathedral, the town: to begin with the very pleasant piazza framing the Duomo front, so different from most such piazze we had visited, since the cathedral was totally dominant while the palazzi played a subsidiary and supportive role. If the tourist office was somewhat casual, a shop nextdoor selling among other things cards and books, provided an extremely civilized substitute, the delightful proprietor giving it an artistic and cultured quality. In contrast, the cafe in the same area, to which we repaired at lunchtime, was a little brash, directly over a wine enoteca - in fact the floor was partly glass above the bottles and barrels - and it featured very prominently photographs of Mussolini's visit to Orvieto on its walls.

Palazzo Populo

A pedestrianized walk to the Piazza de Populo gave access to the Palazzo of the same name, well restored in the local honey-coloured stone. A wide staircase on one side of the facade led to a balcony, which stretched only part way across the front and gave us good views of the town over the roofs; there were still the tell-tale signs from earlier weddings over both balcony and stairs.

ORVIETO
S. ANDREA

PALAZZO COMUNALE,
ORVIETO

Palazzo Comunale & S. Andrea

Another walk between high buildings of Renaissance dates led to the Piazza della Republica, where the symmetrical facade of the Palazzo Comunale faced onto a small square while a Renaissance loggia held one of the finest possible displays of flowering plants for sale: the colours of the cyclamen and even myriads of flowering cacti lit up the dark stone walls. Here, too was the tall dodecagonal campanile of San Andrea, a great Romanesque tower of brick. Inside, the church was simple with tall grey monolithic columns and Corinthian-style capitals, a basilica with a double transept, now sleeping after its medieval historic pageantry when Popes proclaimed crusades and crowned kings of Jerusalem in it.

San Giovanale

Our walk took us on through streets with more and more of a medieval feel, built from the local tufa, towards the Chiesa di S. Giovanale. We were now moving onto one of the promontories of the city rock, above a very steep descent out; there were views across old roofs back towards the Duomo and more excitingly away across the valley to the west and north, extraordinary eroded rifts preceding the craggy slopes of the other side. We reached the eleventh century church, simple and severe on the outside, open and inside prepared for the Saturday evening mass. It was old, and both felt and looked just that. Many of the pillars were held together by metal bands round them. All around, on walls and pillars were frescoes or fragments of frescoes, painted in days before the great artists of the guidebooks, mostly primitive but rich in history, curiously preserved. Despite the fact that everything in the church gave the impression that it was only just still standing, it was clearly loved, cared for and a true place of worship: the priest was hovering in the background. The beginnings of the church date far back, architecturally it is a total muddle, of crumbling grey stone, particularly appropriate on this volcanic rock of Orvieto.

Time was running out for visiting more sites although we knew of other churches and museums. We were not disappointed as we walked back, alternately between old medieval walls, Renaissance fronts leading to courtyards reminiscent of the elegance of a past age, heavy stone facades, past the magnificent cathedral front again and even taking in a little church on the way, one not mentioned in guidebook or map, with an attractive early sixteenth century painting just to remind us that everywhere here was history and beauty. Finally we were off, down the funicular before the winter sun set. The Etruscan or Roman foundations of the city were not to be studied now. They merged into the geology of that extraordinary natural tower on which, as we looked back, the immense body of the cathedral slowly faded into the darkness.

MONTELEONE D'ORVIETO

Monteleone

We knew this small town was perched above the Val di Chiana, on the east side, and that it had little to make the guidebooks notice it. Locally it has a big reputation because of the festivities which go on at Easter time, when many of its inhabitants dress up rather as in a medieval miracle play. We parked just outside the inevitable gateway set between massive towers in the walls. From here the main street dropped gently for three or four hundred metres to the end of the escarpment. All the buildings felt old, even if most were more or less restored. There was a mixture of stone and brick on this Umbrian Tuscan border. The main church, part way down the street, had an Umbrian picture or two of the time of Raphael in it, but it was the scene of a funeral to which a fair number of the inhabitants had gone as well as a number of people from Rome. This rather gave us the reality of the living, and the dying, of the present town more than disappointing us because we were deprived of a picture or two.

A little further, the small widening of the street into a piazza gave view of some quite elegant brick community buildings. Farther still, the road ended in a balustrade looking over the valley, a wonderful view towards Monte Cetona; and here we met the incessant attentions of a very talkative kitten, and soon of two small children as well. From the corner of the piazza, a small track led down the hillside through a reconstructed brick gateway, over the edge of the promontory on which the town was built. A cart was being drawn slowly up through the ranks of the olive trees. We found an alternative way to return along a back alley right on the edge of the old wall, along the north side of the promontory; we looked down on the terraces of olives as we walked past the old houses interspersed often but irregularly with "mini-tunnels" constructed through the buildings back up to the main street. Wood stores or hanging washing completed the picture of the back end of tenements which cannot have altered all that much from medieval times, except that wherever there was the slightest space, through tunnels, up steps or round narrow corners modern cars could drive and were parked.

CASTEL DI FIORE

Nearby to Monteleone, and on the same day, Castel di Fiore provided the goal of a gentle walk across a stream and up the hill side. I had the strong impression of being back as a child walking in the woods of mid-Wales, in the same mixture of rock, moss, scrub and mature trees with streamlets flowing across or beneath the track. At the summit the road straightened along a ridge, past two or three modern houses up to a medieval tower, gateway and walls. This scene just needed three or four horsemen to trot towards the gateway to provide the starting scene for a historical drama; instead, an old Fiat raced past us and was parked just outside the gateway. The place was just a hamlet now, where a few families lived in well-restored houses among the total ruins of many more.

Just inside the gateway, the road widened slightly into a piazza on one side of which was a dramatic and relatively modern sculpture of Saint Michael, the patron saint of

the small church on the other side. The garish nineteenth
century image and the semi-ruined medieval world met
in strange conjunction. There really was only one street,
with a tower at either end, the smaller one next to the
gateway we had entered. Apparently the hamlet had only
ever had the one gate; even though some of the walls
were no longer standing, it was clear where they had been
and there were no signs of any other exits.

The tower at the far end was more of a keep and had at
some time, probably early this century, been partially
restored; there were even signs of old telephone lines to
it, but now it was falling back to its ruinous state. Entry
would have been by steps from outside but now it looked
dangerous. A few crenellations remained at the top, giving
some indication of its past might and it was still worthy
of the modern floodlights, which gave dramatic effect
especially from a distance. The totally ruined house next
door had been bought, but would it ever be restored?
The whole of Castel di Fiore seemed utterly deserted,
waiting for something to happen; then two old ladies
emerged from respective houses for a discussion,
disappeared back in again and the desolation was restored.
Even more than other places we visited among the hills,
right away from civilization it seems, but actually it is
still quite alive presumably because it is reasonably
accessible by car. Its inhabitants could go off during the
day, leave it deserted as we found, earn their living and
return for the night or weekend. By car also visitors from
nearby towns or villages must come together for
entertainment and feast-time: outside the walls was a
small park and picnic site, set out with great care and

capable of accommodating three or four times the local population. Castel di Fiori is both a real place of modern life and a romantic image of medieval history.

MONTEGIOVE

Montgiove

Deep in the hills north of Todi and Orvieto is Montegiove, on a site as impressive as any in these Umbrian hills. We visited the area twice, on both occasions being particularly impressed by the castle high on the hill, but our second visit highlighted the dramatic contrast between the old castle reliving its past and the modern and apparently poor village below the walls.

The castle and estate surrounding it were in private hands - we learned later that a group of people from Rome had renovated it and used it as an escape from the city.

Certainly the massive walls and entrance gave one a good sense of a living castle, while the grounds were particularly well kept. As we looked around, the inhabitants were parading above the outer walls with their Sunday lunchtime drinks, while beside us was a woodcutter's lodging, primitive as if little different from medieval times, lived in, one would think, by an Italian who had never seen a city. How wrong we might have been. In contrast, beside the smart approach to the castle, a group of youths kicked a football about using the old lavabo as a goal, an old man worked in his back garden and two women were hanging out their washing even if it was Sunday. The church was open and had been partly restored recently, but nothing inside particularly interested us except for the impression that it had just been used for a service and felt alive.

Just down the road, the contrasts to be found in this area struck us again, very strongly, as we came to the hamlet of Pornello. A large palazzo sat above a small collection of houses. The approach was the site of a small communal park with picnic tables and the remains of a playground, but all now deserted, overgrown and darkened by heavy trees. The big house itself was semi-derelict and the gardens a ruin. Apparently unoccupied, most of the windows were missing, while in the courtyard, entered directly from the lane, weeds were growing through the cobbles. The old carriage-way led up a slope to a gaping hole before it arrived at the stables. Yet beside these stables one single section of the ruins had been retained as a dwelling with an incongruously smart front door beside broken windows and cracked stone. Apart from this, for the moment at least, the old site was drifting into disappearance. Just down the lane below the old palazzo, a farmhouse had been modernised and extended with a group of modern cottages attached. Maybe the future for this site was not as bad as first impressions indicated, and possibly the ghosts of the old great house would not have it all their own way.

GREPPOLISCHIETTO

Greppolischietto

The route between Montegiove and Greppolischietto to the north, tested out our car's mechanics to the full and not just because of the ruts and portholes. We had to cross a ravine, down and then up severe slopes and round extreme corners. Even in this cultivated and long inhabited land of Central Italy we could find ourselves exploring in countryside that at any moment could feel wild and deserted, as primitive as its buffalo, certainly "light years" away from our modern civilization.

Greppolischietto is a very long name for a tiny hamlet, in itself of no special interest unless one is looking for the flavour of Umbrian countryside. The small group of houses can only be approached on white roads although from the north the road has been improved recently because of a gravel pit part way along. On a fine day at the very beginning of February, we were allowed our first long look at the length of the snow-covered Sybilline hills on the horizon as we parked beside a stone wall in the sunshine. There is here the remnant of a fortified wall, two or three farm houses and a collection of cottages around the church, all pulled tight together as if huddling to keep warm. The modern element was imposed on us as we found the only lane through was blocked by a JCB digging a channel. But in any case we could not become too romantic about the place as a scrappy line of washing interposed straight across the old walls; we were accosted by a man who could only be called the village idiot.

From Greppolischietto we were able to go for a walk up the ridge to the west, bordered by views on both sides, with little sign of human life until we came across a small holding, with three horses grazing. More telling were the three old German cars parked beside the lane. We had heard stories of German alternative style families finding their life out here. The sun was tempting out a number of butterflies even in February, birds, including a pair of firecrests, were singing in the bushes as we climbed further into deep rough forest. We found that the walks like this one on the Umbrian hills, interspersed among our cultural and historical visits, made a wonderfully complete picture of the "green heart of Italy". On our return route we met an Italian who showed us the exotic funghi he was collecting, the largest of which was the size of a dinner plate.

PIETRAFITTA

Pietrafitta

Pietrafitta was one of our local villages, dismissed for a long time as having nothing of special interest, until we stopped below the houses at the spot named on the map as Abbazie delle Sette Fratti. We arrived in the early evening and the church, whose presence was hidden by inhabited old buildings probably once part of the monastery and which we approached through an arch, seemed shut. But a lovely old man, almost crippled presumably with arthritis, called out for us not to go, and slowly came over. As we found so often, he was very proud of the church he lived next to. He opened up the door and took us in, talking about the building all the time. What must have once been a Romanesque church had clearly been rebuilt a number of times and was terribly marked by the evidence of damp. The uneven floor was apparently regularly flooded, but there was a dignified simplicity in his little church, once that of a monastery.

Then, completely to our surprise, he took us to a door beside the altar and encouraged us to look in and down - obviously he could not come and there was no significant light. But what we found was a small and clearly very old crypt, as apparently so often exists below the churches, even the undistinguished ones, of this area. Gradually our eyes became accustomed to the darkness. Strangely, here there was hardly any sense of dampness, presumably because it was dug out of the rock, while the rest of the church just sat on the edge of the flood plain. We could imagine sacred relics being hidden here among the arches at times when Italy was suffering from invading and marauding troops. Here was a good reminder that in Italy there are ancient remains and things of interest in what appear at first sight to be most unlikely places and we thanked our old guide very much for this unexpected experience.

CHAPTER 3

ITINERARY 3: Assisi, S. Maria degli Angeli, Eremo delle Carceri, Spello, Collepino, Bevagna, Bettona

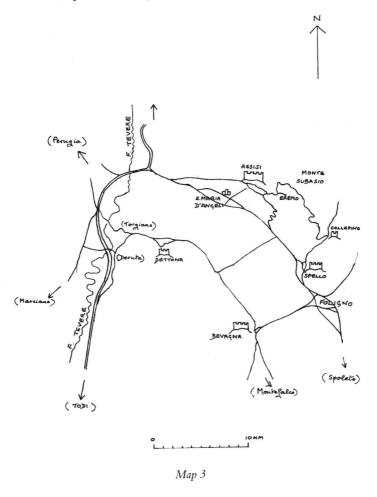

Map 3

ASSISI

So much has been said and written about Assisi and about St. Francis that it seems almost impertinent to add any more; but we visited Assisi five times in three months, Assisi is in Umbria and the "particolari" of Umbria should include our views of this place quite as much as any other. At Assisi, there is almost a conflict between the idea of visiting the art and architecture as a cultural pilgrimage and the truly religious pilgrimage to a spiritual centre honouring the saint. It is not so much that there needs to be such a conflict, but rather that chasing the art can induce a sense of guilt that the religious character is being ignored, while the more cynical person can wonder whether the elaborate churches and commercial developments really do reflect a saint whose emphasis on a life of poverty was such a hallmark. In coming to terms with this dilemma, we were lucky to visit in the first months of the year, since the whole development of tourism or of pilgrimage was not yet really in season. Our visit in January was to an empty Assisi, that in February to one with a small number of visitors but many shops still closed, while by March the place was attractively bursting into life but not yet too crowded. In April we began to see the full season develop. Each visit therefore claimed different details appropriate to the time and weather, while we always found ourselves drawn to S. Francesco before we left Assisi any one day.

S. Francesco and Gateway

The Basilica of S. Francesco is a "Mecca" for Christian pilgrim and artistic tourist alike; equally it is a remarkable place for people watching, as the artists themselves must have done in their own time. Groups are taken around by friars: the Japanese group has a Japanese Franciscan, the intense American party has a very loud and dramatic American friar, the German language invades with another group and the inevitable second Japanese has to make do with a Japanese guide, having presumably run out of Japanese Franciscans. All the speakers have their torches to light up elements of the frescoes, some are clearly very devout while the American is telling of St. Francis zipping here and buzzing there, every story full of modern or slang phrases. Even in January, there were Japanese parties, by later March all nationalities were in on the act: yet most of the time crowds could be avoided and it was possible to stand or sit and stare at these magnificent walls. Individual tourists moved around with all sorts of guide-books, time and time again taking a photo and a flash would appear in the corner of one's vision despite the numerous notices of prohibition. It was odd that when the place was full it was only the friars with their "sermons" who were really making a noise, all others were hushed.

In January, it was a remarkable privilege to be in both the upper and the lower basilica almost alone and certainly in total peace and quiet. Whatever the experts may or may not say about the question of attribution, is this Giotto or not, are these the work of great individual artists or full of assistants' additions, have they been over-restored or not, none of these questions removes the fact that the overall impression is wonderful, not to be found in such entirety anywhere else in Umbria. Each person will find their own highlights: the separate chapel illustrating the story of St. Martin of Tours painted by Simone Martini; the passion stories in one transept of the lower church, the work of Pietro Lorenzetti; the very odd negative impression of the Cimabue crucifixion; the illustration of St. Francis feeding the birds almost hidden in a corner of the upper basilica; or the monumental Madonna and Child with St. Francis, also attributed to Cimabue, in the lower basilica. Lists in guidebooks, depictions of St. Francis in pilgrimage manuals, special significances in the history of art illustration, could go on and on. How odd that so seldom mentioned is the wonderful medieval glass in the lower church.

As we leave the upper basilica in February, we look back at the facade of the church, unfortunately almost covered in scaffolding and we notice a party of Japanese coming out. Everyone of them on the way out puts down his or her camera on the pavement immediately outside the door and goes out ten yards. In time there is a large pile of cameras in the doorway; one Japanese is deputed to stay there while the rest group together. One by one, the lone deputy picks up and uses every single one of the cameras in turn until the last group photograph is taken, at which point the whole party herds back to collect cameras and rushes on to the next site to be visited.

This front of the upper basilica always seemed quieter than the colonnaded piazza lower front, and from here not only can one progress up the main street which runs all the way up through Assisi, but also at the top corner is a very attractive street towards the Porta San Giacomo. Just outside this gate is a small, potentially very useful, carpark at the top of the road leading down the valley behind Assisi to the charming chapel and ancient bridge of Santa Croce dei Galli. Alternatively there is a quiet path, past a German nunnery, leading all the way up to the Rocca, and another useful carpark. A great advantage of this path is that there are views over the roofs down into the town, its churches and towers. Obviously, the other buildings of Assisi are individually minor beside the Basilica of San Francesco, but cumulatively in their pink stone they add up to a magnificent city. We picked out our favourite spots on different occasions.

We saw the church of San Pietro in January. Down by the gate and piazza of the same name, it is a simple church, unpretentious, mainly Romanesque and particularly memorable for the fine facade with three large rose windows. The interior is beautifully bare since the Baroque altars and furniture were apparently removed in a restoration some forty years ago. Probably this would be a fine escape when the Basilica is full of crowds, in a sense back to the time of Saint Francis before his 'glorification'.

the main Piazza

The Piazza del Commune more than anywhere demonstrated the contrast between the cold, bare, bleak and hardly populated January, and the open cafe world where tourists of all nationalities mixed with Italians in the sun of late March. This piazza has fine medieval buildings on both sides of what is really a widened street, with a handsome fountain at the far end. The most famous building here, the pillared facade of the Roman temple of Minerva, is an amazing survival, especially when on inspection the stone looks so terribly fragile. It takes its place in the medieval frontage remarkably naturally, but the baroque interior of the church is a world apart. On the step outside, in March, we sat eating ices, watching enthralled as one Italian spoke to two others using his hands all the time, up, down, praying, thrown wide, shoved in pockets, up to the eyes; were words really necessary? On the same occasion a group of teenage schoolchildren were relaxing, a group of girls in the party, sitting down, looking at photos, jumping up to see friends, sighing and yawning at the effort of it all so typically the teenager, it could be of any nationality during a school trip anywhere in the modern world.

Assisi

We visited, on separate occasions, the two other big churches of Assisi. Santa Chiara was rather a disappointment. The facade is strong with plenty of space in front, where on this occasion oranges were being sold for charity, but inside the church was very dark and bare, like a great cave. There is one special chapel, even darker, holding a beautiful painting and many relics. Santa Chiara is so different from San Francesco, another world it seemed and one in which we did not feel welcome. In contrast San Rufino, the Duomo, seemed much warmer;

it has a fine facade, although when we visited one part of it was always under wraps. Our guess must be that it is the best facade in Assisi to judge from what we could see, but inside there is nothing very special, a large and ornate space. We decided to use a proffered combined ticket, allowing us to view a museum with pictures and the crypt. In both cases, the enjoyment was the greater because the custodiennes were very pleasant and welcoming. The art was interesting to us since we seemed to be trailing Umbrian artists and we had recently seen Dono Doni's home town of Corciano. The crypt was something more special. It is entered from outside San Rufino, is well underneath the present levels around, was beautifully simple Romanesque, much wider than long and containing a Roman sarcophagus whose sculpture seemed doubtfully appropriate for the resting place for a Christian saint. Apparently he is no longer there to be upset by a fine Roman carving of Diana and Endymion. At much the same level as the crypt are the partly reconstructed remains of the cloisters of the Carolingian age, suitably ancient looking. Outside again in the sunlight, we admired the Romanesque campanile and looked up and beyond to the Rocca.

the Rocca

Twice we went to the top of Assisi, in January walking, in March mostly driving, both times in a strong wind. This almost seems to be a different town. We stayed outside the great walls of the fortress, enjoying sunshine and views, watching the various little dramas enacted out by others whiling away the lunchtime period: a French party where nuns were mixing with other religious pilgrims in pleasant friendship; and Italian who drove up at speed with his three guests, fur coats to the fore, and gave them an involved lecture on the history of the Rocca; a young couple, she bored while he took ages to get his photograph just right; children who at last had freedom to clamber around; all, in limbo, waiting for the town of Assisi to open its doors again to the tourist and pilgrim.

Our final visit to Assisi in April took us to far less known streets, exploring parts of the town seldom noticed by the tourists. One of the churches we had not yet visited was the ex-cathedral of Santa Maria Maggiore, downhill from the main Piazza del Commune. We had seen the Romanesque apses and old campanile from above, and now we went inside and found a beautifully simple Romanesque interior, with a raised east end over a crypt. There were remnants of frescoes in a building which must have been well-known to Saint Francis and have remained largely unaffected by the excessive demands of the pilgrimages, saved by being replaced as cathedral by San Rufino.

San Damiano

We called in at S. Damiano on a damp afternoon, wet enough to bring life to colour but not too much to spoil the walk down to the side of the Franciscan monastery, once again in the hands of the friars instead of English aristocrats, as was true for a number of years. Beside the pathway was an olive grove with sheep grazing; they not only ate the grass, but also standing on their hindlegs were eating the lower olive leaves and shoots. The church itself was being restored, but the doors were open and much could be seen. The signposted tour of the convent took us round rooms supposedly dating back to Saint Clare and her successors, showing various sacred mementoes: one's mind starts to go blank. For us the highlight of San Damiano was the cloister, perfectly preserved and now planted out with beautiful flowers. The posted order to preserve Silence here encouraged the peace and reverential calm apparent more in the cloisters than elsewhere in the convent. Off the cloister walk was the refectory which had benches and tables around the room rather than down the middle. There were a number of old frescoes. Even on a wet day, it was a beautiful visit, our last message from Assisi, as we left the courtyard where a couple of Franciscans were quietly talking to a nun.

SANTA MARIA DEGLI ANGELI
ASSISI

Santa Maria degli Angeli

Of the various possible visits just outside Assisi, all linked with its patron saint, we went to just two, the one the grandest, the other the simplest and most remote. Santa Maria degli Angeli became a landmark for us miles around, as much as did the Rocca of Assisi. The visits we made caused us mixed emotions about this immense temple. At Easter time, stalls full of blue and while dresses for children filled the square around the church and emphasised the commercial aspect of a site packed with crowds. In February, it was much more nearly deserted and we were able to feel more charitable. The superlatives of size are obvious: the architecture has a certain strength of grandeur, while the inside is tremendous, the adjective opposite to any one would associate with St. Francis. Extraordinarily incongruous is the little chapel, the Porziuncula, of the time of saint's death; this must be unique in its setting and is really remarkably moving. Surely, Saint Francis would find all of the modern world so far away from his foundation of friars: it is true that the grandeur of the setting is contrary to his life's work, and yet the devotion of the friars and the noticeable reverence of pilgrim, even tourist, cannot be denied. The primitive building of the Porziuncula, the ancient art, the emotional appeal of the memorials to the age of the first Franciscan community live through any incongruity deriving from the massive expense and monumental grandeur of the church around them.

Eremo delle Carceri

We also visited the Eremo delle Carcere in February, almost on our own. Here at last we felt something of the simple other-worldliness and surrounding nature associated with the medieval saint. Some way up Monte Subasio a small entrance with simple notices led down to a group of buildings clinging to the forested slopes. No friars or religious were apparent and yet their presence was quietly everywhere. The tour we followed took us through tiny cells, low arches in between, seeming to lead down almost inside the rock without any sense of plan. Each room had simple objects of devotion, some primitive pictures and a silence to hush a voice. We climbed out of the last cell, up and along a forest pathway around the crevice in which the Eremo is situated. Wooden crosses and a rough wooden altar marked a pilgrim route which doubled up as a forest and nature wander. The quiet of the middle of the day in the trees on the mountain slope gave a permanency to the buildings clinging to the other side of the dark ravine, themselves now in sunshine; another couple walked on through the forest tracks apparently intent on the environmental qualities rather than the peculiarly religious. One could just stop here completely, so that the phrase "to tear ourselves away" expressed a physical effect when we eventually decided to walk away but not to forget.

Eremo delle Carceri

SPELLO

We first met the town of Spello in January, the winter sun clearly above but the mist hanging in the valley. Parking below and outside the town gave access to two alternative arch entrances, the smaller of which the vehicles use to ascend into the town. The larger, the Porta Consolare, one of five Roman gateways, now pedestrianised and the subject of excavations outside, provides a magnificent entry in almost white stone to a city dominated by the rose-coloured Mount Subasio rock. Three statues, possibly representing members of a family either welcome you or stand above the arch on protective guard, depending on the attitude of the moment. From here one main street curves its way more or less right up steeply towards the Rocca area high on the hill. Two thirds of the way up there is one main piazza, or widening of the street: here there are no magnificent palazzi, rather medieval remains patched into more modern fronts. On the ascent, rather dull facades cover two fine churches on the right both containing special art.

Spello

In the first of these, Santa Maria Maggiore, we were welcomed by the custodian standing by his stall of cards and books from which we bought, since the information office of Spello had been elusive and once found, firmly shut. On the left of the nave we found the Capella Baglioni, painted on all three sides and the vaults by Pinturicchio. Access was shut off by a grill which particularly affected the viewing of the two sides. Light was only provided by slipping 1,000 L notes into the appropriate machine: we could not help wondering at such sophistication here that a note could activate it, and whether some other note-like paper would work as well. The end result was well worth the money, although we used three notes fully to view the Annunciation, with the dove zooming down to the Virgin, the wall of whose house was decorated with a self-portrait of the artist; the Adoration of the Child Jesus with many very real people and a fantastic rocky background; and finally the Disputation in the Temple, possibly the most interesting with even more obvious portraits, one of the prior Troilo

Baglioni, commissioner of the frescoes, two oddly-proportioned children in front of the crowd and an idealistic Renaissance temple dominating the background. The main impression was of a richness, wonderful colours and a beautifully balanced composition in all three pictures.

And the rest of the church. One wondered whether there was anything else we really wanted to see after the Pinturicchio chapel, in this rather too elaborate Baroque ensemble. But in truth, many items were worth noting, including on both sides of the apse, two frescoes by Perugino: this allowed us continue our "trail" of the local artist, even if the frescoes were of a late date. They had a special beauty in their not over-restored pastel shades. Our attention was then drawn by the very friendly and obviously proud custodian: perhaps we had shown we were worth his extra attention. He left his stall and took us to the Canons Room off the north transept and showed another Pinturicchio, a Madonna and Child which was to our eyes beautiful expecially in its simple and private setting, and the figures were very alive.

Spello

We moved on up the main street, to San Andrea, the second church for us to see, a simple thirteenth-century facade fronting a dark, much frescoed church, apparently of little artistic interest. But this impression was unfair. Immediately inside, on the left, is a curious little baptistry chapel, frescoed almost all over, dating from the fifteenth century. The work was that of a local artist, possibly primitive but charming in its overall effect. A resurrection garden with painted or artificial flowers "planted" all over the floor of the chapel could have been "naf" in the extreme, but somehow it fitted in. The second feature to strike one was the large crucifix, above the high altar, apparently from the school of Giotto, simple without the additional pictures often found on the arms and ends, except for a Franciscan kneeling at the feet of Jesus, a miniature: the whole effect was of suffering without the over-dramatic blood-pouring that sometimes appears.

The further treasures of the church were not clear until a priest slipped in from a side door, welcomed us and immediately started putting lights on, talking to us about the transepts and their contents. On the right was a magnificent Pinturicchio picture of the Madonna and saints, partly painted by assistants, full of colour and this time fully visible, unobstructed by grille or glass. Again, a young child, the youthful John the Baptist, took the attention among the rather sober saints. In the left transept, apparently newly found was a set of early frescoes of which our priest was clearly very proud. They are now placed on a framework, free-standing. They had been behind the heavy altar in the transept, but its restoration had led to the discovery of these simple beautiful frescoes hidden for years behind the reredos.

After a coffee in a bar shared by school teenagers and local policemen, we walked up as far as possible, ending at a closed Franciscan church below the Rocca, with a viewpoint to reward the climber. The mist still obstructed distant views, but Mount Subasio dominated over a prospect of roads, cars, houses, olives, all in miniature. The remains of the ancient amphitheatre could be seen but we were not tempted to make the trip: we could see it much better from above. Halfway down again, farther on the side of Spello towards Assisi, we came to our second Roman gateway, the Porta Venere. It was difficult to be certain what was Roman and what was Medieval, especially since there were two tall dodecagonal towers flanking the arch of apparently mixed origin. Did it really matter? The overall effect was ancient, but more significantly to us, made a beautiful and proportioned ensemble evocative of this medieval city of coloured stone, and relatively unspoilt by modern times.

We made a second visit to Spello in March and added a few more details as well as seeing the Pinturicchio and Perugino works again. We had by now become more aware of Dono Doni, whose birthplace in Corciano we had seen. In San Andrea, Spello, the same priest whom we had seen before and who had shown us the picture treasures, was now just as enthusiastic and proud. He pointed out that the Doni picture here was apparenrly unique: Joseph was acknowledging Mary as mother-to-be. But the picture by the same painter in S. Lorenzo, which we entered on this visit, was dark, dirty and almost impossible to view: there were no lights in sight. This church was a mass of Baroque adornment, not to our taste, all in a church whose facade is a muddle of dates, parts and windows all over the place.

In total contrast, a very smart and superbly appointed gallery up the road was devoted to the modern artist of Spello, Norberto. A sophisticated and obviously bored young lady sat at the desk while we wandered through room after room below street level. The pictures showed many earlier styles but those in his present style, for sale in most places in the area, have towers and houses built up, just like Spello, and little monks running round the scenes doing all manner of extraordinary things. The streets we saw, especially off the main street above Via Tempi Diana, or the views of Spello from the roads in the valley are so clearly the inspiration for or are reflected in his work. The painting is kept very simple and flat, with repeated images in the houses, churches, gateways, towers and fields, either in the summer or, as he likes to do so often, with a winter covering of snow. But what makes the work so appealing is the sense of humour transmitted particularly by the little monk figures, on the march up a street, leaning out of windows, in the middle of a field of corn reaping it from the centre outwards, bringing their bicycles to be mended or putting on the lights all over the town. The colours used are simple, primary, but this is not the work of a primitive artist but of one who had achieved a superb medium for the love of his world, that of Spello in particular.

COLLEPINO

Collepino

A steady climb up the road from Spello, rising over three hundred more metres, through terraced olive groves brought us to Collepino. The village is sited, overlooking a deep valley leading into the hills, at the point where the white road zigzags up onto the upper reaches of Monte Subasio. Collepino is one of the villages where the local government - we were told, the local Communists - has clearly embarked on major restoration of village life, in this case well in progress at the time of our visit. The end result is a very pleasing mixture of ancient monument and clean newly finished stone house and pavement, all in the local pink and white. Though the car park is above and leads onto a castle mound, the suitable approach is from slightly below through the restored village archway, into a maze of streets varying between wide steps and narrow paveways. It is almost an advantage that there is no particular work of art or church building to be looked for, the church itself being a simple structure, so that the whole village becomes a work of art in itself. There are stone benches outside the houses, flower containers in suitable places, corner vistas to surprise every few yards, a successful restaurant here, a down-to-earth line of washing there, and every moment or two a view down hill into the valley or across to the hills southwards.

In the centre of the village, a precise spot difficult to locate for certain in this maze of streets, the old town hall was at this moment a building site. Four workmen mixed and placed concrete, unusually working right through lunchtime. The ruins of the present gave little idea of what had been the palazzo, but one hoped that a new version of the medieval village podesta would be erected to complete the reconstituted image. The builders gave the impression they were enjoying working on the centre of our work of art, a modern version of the woodcut images of a Renaissance building works. Immediately above the concrete mixer was the remnant wall of the old keep, while all the time the towering mass of Subasio overlooked us, the white track snaking its way up through trees and scrub.

BEVAGNA

Bevagna

We came to Bevagna at the gate of the town leading to the Piazza Garibaldi, quite late on a fine Sunday morning. Just in time, as it turned out. The town has hardly spread outside the medieval walls in modern times and is quite remarkable for Umbria: it is flat. We walked straight through the main thoroughfare, knowing that we should make for the Piazza Silvestri, as the main square is called, and found it an almost perfect medieval Romanesque setting, three church facades and a town hall set at different angles around the open space. We were just in time to catch the late Italian Sunday morning parade, in the winter sunshine, ladies in their best fur coats, some accompanying incongruous mini-skirts, the men in Sunday funeral best, winter coats and usually hats. Groups of five to ten chatted, dispersed to attach themselves to other groups and began again. Suddenly, almost as if the school bell had been rung, the groups re-asseembled and moved off in different directions, clearly home and to lunch. Within just minutes the piazza was almost empty.

Bevagna Piazza

We could now study the architectural content of the place. Quite near the steps up to the entrance of the Palazzo dei Consoli was a single column, with the remains of a Corinthian-type capital, the Column of S. Rocco: a reminder that this was once a Roman city. The palazzo is simple and plain, leaving the drama to the two main church facades. The smaller of the two, S. Silvestro, seemed truncated as if it was meant to have a tower on the right, but someone never built it. Its only door reflected the main door of the larger S. Michele Arcangelo, both Romanesque with pinkish marbled circuits in between the curved and carved arches of the facade. This church of San Michele does have a tower on the right, two storeys of Romanesque openings surmounted by a small spire. Dominating the front above the main door, was a gaping hole, not a true rose window, but as if the window should have been there, carved all round. In fact the truth is that in the eighteenth century they had punched a plain rose window into the facade, without any tracery or decoration. All these buildings gave the piazza an aura of medieval stolidity, an impression of a light grey stone stage waiting for a coloured pageant. The fountain was a nineteenth century addition but luckily it is also grey, simple and spoiled nothing of the effect.

inside church

Inside the churches ancient architecture took over, almost monolithic, weathered and wizened; whatever fittiings there were had little effect. Both S. Silvestro and S. Michele have the same sort of construction, a nave leading up a large number of steps to an apse with the altar high above, while at each side are steps down to a crypt fitted in below the sanctuary. The church of S. Michele is larger and its tall pillars clearly owe much to Roman times. The smaller, S. Silvestro, hardly seems to be used for services, almost redundant, and yet to us was the more perfect. Here the pillars have twelfth-century capitals carved into forms which are of an Egyptian order supposedly copied from some Roman remains. This is one place where the building looks and feels older than the accepted date of construction. Both churches are the work of the same mason: in the the case of S. Silvestro, the date of the building, 1195, and the name of the builder, Binello, is given on the facade. The church both looked and felt ancient, especially down in the crypt. We wondered if we might be locked in, and for how long and how many ghosts we might see. In fact, almost as soon as we had walked out again into the piazza, the doors of both churches were locked and I am sure no-one checked if any visitor was still down in a crypt.

The walk round the rest of the town was pleasant, if not dramatic. On both occasions we were in Bevagna, now and a month later, we were continually accosted by a mentally-deficient wanderer. It was difficult not to feel that some such must be the necessary accompaniment to such an ancient place, a Roman ghost lingering through medieval times. Behind S. Silvestro and the Palazzo dei Consuli was a sunny open space showing off both buildings in a lighter vein. Much of the old town wall was still standing, and it directed the walk around. At one point in the eastern part we came across a group of old and even partly derelict dwellings, set on a curve, the remains of part of the circumference of the Roman amphitheatre, reminding us of the dramatic example at Lucca. We did not try to see the Roman mosaic and other treasures: probably they would have been closed. But we had completed our visit; it needed no more to make a perfect medieval Sunday occasion.

Bevagna Piazza

We made our second visit to Bevagna on a weekday. The market stall just outside the town gateway offered porchetta from the side of a mobile van - could one imagine a medieval butcher here? On this occasion the whole town was more lively, a different feeling engendered compared with the Sunday, but even so peace and quiet was only just off the main streets. A positive advantage was that two places, previously closed to us, were open: the church of S. Domenico and the Palazzo dei Consoli. The former was a pleasant friary hall church, made for preaching, with some late Baroque fittings and a few early fresco fragments; it is the Gothic and later complement to the two Romanesque churches of the piazza.

Just before we mounted the staircase of the Palazzo, a group of older primary schoolchildren came running down; as we entered four Italians were packing up their props, the end of an extended lesson, a good example of modern educational use of facilities belonging to the past. Clearly the performance had been contemporary even if the stage was not. We went upstairs and inside was a perfect little nineteenth century theatre. A remarkably large stage was faced by a small stalls section surrounded by three circles one above the other, of boxes each containing two smaller and two taller chairs, each box a miniature theatre in itself. Everywhere the gold leaf on the wood was complemented by plush red velvet material in very good condition. Right up at the top, "the gods", a balustrade completed this charming and actively used theatre from a previous age, an unexpected find inside the sober palazzo on that most beautiful of Romanesque piazzas.

BETTONA

Bettona

Bettona is set high on its hill above the road between Torgiano with its wine and Bevagna which had become well-known to us for Romanesque churches. For some time there seemed little point in going all the way up to the town as we passed by to other places. Thank goodness, in the end we did and were rewarded with an excellent three hour visit. It seemed easiest to park on the road set on the ramparts round the old walls and to walk up into the village, in this case by way of steps beside the crypt on one of the old churches, through the cellars of the houses in the old walls. This approach took us from a view across towards Assisi as an outsider beside the walls, through the darkness of a tunnel to emerge into the sunlight of an insider visitor to the historic site of the main piazza.

Two great church masses, the Palazza del Podesta now a pinacoteca, a more modern if still old Comunale building and a number of smaller family palazzi formed an irregular piazza peopled by the requisite strolling old men, ever ready with smiles. One of the palazzi took our attention, as that of the Baglioni, in particular of one Malatesta IV, count of Bettona, a leading member of the family whose history so dominated Perugia and the surrounding area for hundreds of years as we were continually reminded almost wherever we went. The proud plaque on this faded palazzo referred to Malatesta, who died on 24 December 1531, aged thirty-nine, as captain general of Venice and Florence, possibly at different times, one of the series of condottieri who fill the history books. It said that he died here in this palazzo and appropriately we saw his portrait in the pinacoteca. This gallery provided us with a treat. The Palazzo del Podesta was, as normal, decorated, or almost more correctly annotated, with the shields of the coats of arms of the various governors of Bettona over the ages. Entry was by way of a flight of steps at one end, the medieval part. The pinacoteca we found inside had only been opened four months previously and today we were the only visitors. The curator was a young lady who not only welcomed us but was so pleased to tell us about both the gallery and the pictures themselves: she was very clearly a considerable expert in her own right. We were told that the pictures had belonged here for some time, at least since the turn of the century, but the best of them had been stolen. Hereby hung a story, somewhat obscure in detail, of professional theft involving members of government some years ago as well as the mafia, and the recovery recently of most of the paintings which had just "turned up" in Jamaica. Some had been damaged when stolen by being cut out of their frames or mounts, but now most are restored and returned to form a small but attractive local collection of art.

Some of the iconography of the fourteenth to sixteenth century religious painting had become clear to us from seeing so much over the past weeks, but the young lady here informed us of many more details, helping us to make so much more sense of what we had already seen and were to see in the next weeks. At Bettona, two particular paintings took our notice, not so much for special artistic quality, but rather for the imagery. For the first time we saw, or at least now noticed, a picture of the Madonna and Child from the school of Perugino, with St. Anne who with her outstretched cloak was protecting the other figures from the arrows of the Redeemer. A very strange concept and one we would have liked to have understood better, though we did not see this particular imagery again. The other picture to notice was one by Jacopo Siculo, Sicilian but employed in this area on a number of occasions, of a group of six saints, two of whom were unidentifiable, with between and above them a representation of the town of Bettona; as we had pointed out to us, and could see for ourselves as we left the town later, this was a view of the town quite clearly recognisable as the present Bettona, not just the one of the late fifteenth century. Jacopo Siculo had clearly been here and looked carefully at the view of Bettona which has changed little, whereas the follower of Perugino, a local man, had in another picture painted the town from memory, and not very well or with a poor memory. Because the curator had been so helpful, this gallery visit was one of our most enjoyable even if the material presented was not particularly outstanding.

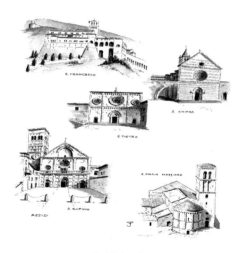

Assisi churches

CHAPTER 4

ITINERARY 4: Castelleone, Collazzone, S. Terenziano, Montefalco, Foligno, Sassovivo, Trevi, Spoleto, Narni, Amelia, Carsulae

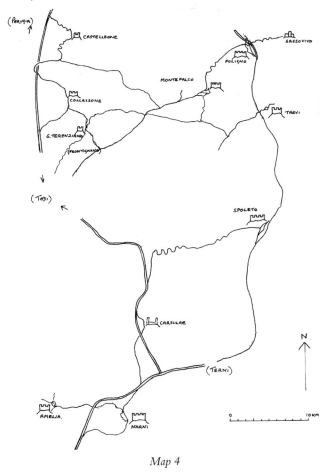

Map 4

CASTELLEONE

Castelleone

A little village on the slopes above Deruta, looking down
over the Tevere valley, Castelleone is a miniature medieval
moment in time. Almost totally surrounded by ancient
walls, it has a grid of two roads crossing at the centre,
and a gateway entrance only east and west. Parking
outside, we entered by the eastern arch and found olive
oil inside! To the right was a large emporium of olive oil,
the street was named "olive oil" and notices everywhere
proclaimed the raison d'etre of the village. The emporium
was effectively a palazzo, attached to the tower of the
gatehouse, with a fine shaded garden outside the walls.
Hardly anyone was about but the few there were greeted
us in a very friendly way.

The church at the other end of the main street was in
good condition, open and clearly the object of much care
and attention. Most of the facade and the decoration
inside were simple late Renaissance or early Baroque;
there were also frescoes by the fifteenth century Umbrian
artist, Matteo da Gualdo, which even if not very great

art, were treasures in such an unexpected and tiny place. This is a feature which makes Umbria such a special area. The art seems to belong so completely, in the church for which it was originally painted and as loved now as then, part of the village centre of worship instead of just an item in a specialist gallery.

COLLAZZONE

Collazzone

The route to Collazzone was truly one of contrast, the absolute flat of the Tevere valley on a straight road across compared with the winding climb up the hills immediately south east to this old town-village, one of those in process of becoming beautifully looked after. The great yellow cranes were out, the blue shutes for rubbish, the cement mixers churning away, converting the old houses in the town walls into modern apartments. The slopes up to the place and the views from it alternate

107

between large cultivated areas of olive trees or oaks and pines in forest clumps serrated by barren land. The road out continues for a mile or so along the ridge which then drops away in all directions.

Collazzone

The link between Collazzone and Todi is a close one, both in its present organisation and in its history, especially in the person of the poet and mystic Jacopone de Benedetti, the ardent follower of St. Francis more usually called just Jacopone da Todi, who was too ascetic even for the mainstream of that order of friars. His feast is particularly celebrated in Collazzone for it was here that he came to die: his feast is on 14 April, though he died on Christmas day. We wandered the little streets and the medieval gateways, saw the outside of the Convento di S. Lorenzo where Jacopone died and the restored palazzo townhall, all very quiet, apart from the building work, on a weekday morning. In particular, the old gate with steps leading up to it, a covered walkway round the corner underneath a great tower, recently restored with machicolations, suggests the atmosphere of the medieval.

The parish church of S. Lorenzo was built on the foundations of the old castle and in itself is dignified, but nothing special. Inside is a strange treasure which quite clearly the present day inhabitants of Collazzone revere as much as did the medieval. Inside it is not immediately obvious; the church is pleasant while the chapel to the south of the chancel at first just seems beautifully kept, decorated with fresh flowers and candles. Deep into the chapel, behind glass and protected therefore one hopes from theft, is the primitive carving that is their treasure, a polychrome wooden Madonnna and Child dating back probably to the fourteenth century. It is set in its 'house', back, sides and roof, constructed and painted two or three centuries later. The Christ Child looks like a doll, the feet of the Madonna are large and square, the crown looks more like a helmet and the colours show no shades of values, but even so it is a wonderful example, a rare survival outside museums of what must have been a time and place where art and faith met without thinking there was any difference

S. TERENZIANO

Above the Tevere

This little village on the hills above the Tevere was not expecially distinguished but rather typical, sited around the expected historic centre, in this case a flat, walled area entered through one gate only from the modern piazza with its cafe, shop and small park. This old part has one street down its length and several side streets on one side only, all leading to dead ends. Some of the houses were renovated but most were not, having a dark grey and dank air this cool February afternoon. At the far end was what must at one time have been a magnificent palazzo occupying the whole end of the walled village. But, made largely of the typical disintegrating grey sandstone, it seemed only a matter of time for the whole place to collapse and die. There were no churches here; they were well outside the walls. We visited one, beautifully kept, retaining elements of the Romanesque, with an underground church immediately below and a number of seventeenth and eighteenth century paintings inside.

What made S. Terenziano memorable was our coffee stop, in the pleasant bar just outside the old gate. As we entered we saw there were at least a dozen Italian men all round one table, four playing cards, the others watching, and absolute silence. The whole time we were there, no-one bought anything or drank anything, the cafe was just their meeting-place. The silence continued until suddenly the game of cards ended and everyone erupted: everyone shouted, giving his estimation of what had or should have happened, who did or did not play the right cards, everyone talking so that surely no-one could have heard anything said. Almost as suddenly all the noise stopped, one of the four playing dealt the next hand and the next game began. Four more men came in and joined the group and all spectators stood behind, watching intently, nodding or grimacing. Silence again. All were intent on the game while further back two older men played their own game. Just as suddenly the eruption came again, all shouting excitedly, young and old, tidy and untidy, everyone totally involved. Clearly this pattern would go on well into the afternoon: we found it hard to drag ourselves away to continue our wander around the local hills which as well as being peopled by rows of cypresses were dotted all over with spectacular remains of medieval castles, some of which had been impressively rebuilt or restored. It is an area that we might well have explored in more detail if other nearer and more famous sites had not occupied us.

near Frontignano

MONTEFALCO

Another Umbrian walled town set on a hill, a landmark for miles around and a viewpoint with a balcony panorama of the vale of Foligno, the small old city is far enough up the slopes that parking outside the ancient wall led to just a short climb to the centre. We knew of the artistic treasures to be seen, but the town itself, charming as it is in a broken-down sort of way, seemed so much more provincial than its neighbours of Assisi, Spello, Spoleto or even Bevagna. Obviously the art came by historical chance in a way: famed artists from Florennce were emlpoyed here, but equally local artists were also inspired to make their own significant contribution. We needed to hurry to get to the art museum of San Francisco before the inevitable hiatus of the middle of the day, so we postponed viewing other parts of the town.

Montefalco Piazza

A modern purpose-built annex beside an austere facade, manned by friendly personnel, together with a fine selection of books for sale and efficient lockers for banned cameras to be stored, was an unlikely preparation for the immediate impact of the church next door. On first entry, this ex-chiesa seemed immense, clearly a hall designed for mass preaching to the populace, and now dauntingly full of paintings and frescoes in all directions: we had entered from the side. An art critic could write a book of analysis and assessment of value, but we simply drank in the beauty, whatever the so-called status of the particular artists. The special glory and impact must be the apse of the church with a complete cycle of frescoes, concerning the life of St. Francis, by Benozzo Gozzoli, possibly not the most highly rated of Florentine artists, but here unexpectedly far from Florence producing beautiful figures with simple fresh colours and fascinating local backgrounds. Certainly there were great advantages for our fullest appreciation when visiting out of season this rather less well known site: we were totally on our own, as if on a private viewing; and because the lighting was so good over the whole apse the cycle could be viewed from one stance, a benefit too often impossible. The views of Arezzo, Bevagna and Montefalco itself were clearly recognizable once pointed out by appropriate notes provided. In a sense, while one knew this idea to be heretical in the extreme, the series of frescoes here brought the story of St. Francis into our own range of appreciation more than the great Giotto series of Assisi.

In this amazing church, and also in the little gallery attached, there was so much more to be seen, wonderfully at leisure, whether the work of supposedly great artists or not did not seem to matter. The whole impression of this building, even if technically a museum, gave some insight into what a late medieval church of this area must have been like, a living art-treasure of worship. There were other frescoes by Gozzoli, some beautiful Madonnas by Tiberio d'Assisi and remarkable vault frescoes by Giovanni di Corraduccio, smaller frescoes on many of the pillars together with a Nativity scene by Perugino on an apse at the west end. This last with its typical Trasimeno-like blue and brown background scene and well-spaced figures allowed us to continue our following of this so very Umbrian artist.

After this magnificent art collection we wandered in the rest of Montefalco: streets up and around the hilltop, steps and cobbles, a wonderfully rich stone now decorated with flower pots. Our walk took us around brick stepped streets eventually to Porta Frederica II, both providing a magnificent view and the reminder in its broken medieval walls of the Barbarossa's conquering impact on this part of Umbria. We returned to the Piazza del Comune, nothing compared with that of Todi or Bevagna, maybe, but a charming whole, with the Palazzo Comunale of rather uncertain style holding one side together without dominating as so often in such piazzas, and another ex-church, now a theatre, providing a Renaissance facade unusual in Umbria. Coffee in a wine bar, elegantly on the square, gave us time to appreciate the peace; it was clearly more sophisticated than some of our coffee stops, with smart Italians drinking and reading papers.

Montefalco tower gateway

Santa Chiara was closed on its secrets, but the road led us on to Sant' Illuminata with a triple-arched Renaissance portico, opening into a dark church full of frescoes. The artist was Francesco Melanzio, working in or about 1500, a man of this city and producing here an ensemble in the five chapels on both sides of the church which was more than just competent. We had already seen the work of this artist in the gallery, one of the extraordinary Madonna del Soccorso pictures, an iconography particular to Umbria, illustrating a story easily transferred to a modern estate, that of a young mother casually invoking the devil to deal with her unruly child, now in a panic when he appears so to do, now desperately calls for the Virgin.

Before leaving Montefalco completely, we made the short trip to the Monasterio di San Fortunato, more in hope than expectation, to see more frescoes. The little Franciscan monastery is set about a mile outside the town in an ilex wood; the gate to the courtyard was open and yes, we could visit the church. It was more than just a visit; we were shown round with all the enthusiasm of a devotee by a Franciscan monk, who came from Sri Lanka, had spent time in Croydon and who was so pleased to talk to us, and it did not strain our weakness in Italian! In the church were faded angels over the entrance door and another fresco inside, both by Gozzoli, who had clearly been busy when visiting Montefalco. The subject, Saint Fortunato himself, was very truly present and we were shown his bones laid out below the fresco, a saint living the best part of a thousand years before St. Francis, but clearly the Franciscans have a wonderful veneration for him. After a very full tour of the church, our friend took us across the courtyard and unlocked the Capella delle Rose, almost an alcove of a chapel covered in frescoes by Tiberio d'Assisi, who painted at much the same time as Gozzoli but was native to this area. We were given a very beautiful moment here in the peaceful setting of an active Franciscan monastery. It had been a wonderful artistic sight but more, a privilege to be able to visit the convent, on our own with such a sympathetic Franciscan guide. A moment we would long savour, Montefalco had indeed revealed to us some special treasures.

FOLIGNO

Foligno

In a sense we missed out at Foligno, never quite sure whether to visit or not. It is quite a large industrial site and did not encourage us to wander. The one time we did go there was not with the idea of making a special visit but we were on the way to Sassovino. We arrived at Foligno about lunchtime and apart from entering at just the moment when all the teenagers from apparently the whole of Umbria were coming out of school or college, we found the centre quiet in the March sunshine.

The cathedral is much restored on the outside but still showed us two magnificent facades, one west, the other south, next to each other except for a house firmly fixed between the two. These two facades included some of the best Romanesque decorative carving we were to see in Umbria. It seems that the architect of the two churches in Bevagna had been at work also at Foligno, but the decoration here was much more elaborate, including various mosaic designs, signs of the zodiac paralleling the symbols of the evangelists and the images of a king and bishop, apparently Barbarossa and the local bishop of Foligno. Here Barbarossa was associated with fine carving instead of with destruction at Montefalco. All was especially fine in the sunshine; we did not feel particularly deprived that the doors of the cathedral were firmly shut. These facades faced into the large and irregular main piazza on which was one of the largest of the town halls in the area, dramatically developed from the older one last century. This sunny piazza contrasted with the route we took around the other side of the cathedral, in dark and dingy streets, quite old but rundown and miserable. There seemed little to keep us after an ice-cream in the sun.

SASSOVIVO

Sassovivo

Often leaving a large town for a small place is difficult. We had planned to visit the abbey of Sassovivo beyond Foligno but signposts did not seem to help and we found ourselves in a suburb village way off the right direction and stopped to study the map. Almost at once a young Italian on a moped stopped and asked, in quite good English, which way we wanted to go. We explained and he immediately suggested that we followed him in the car while he led us to the right road. Not only was this so kind, he also seemed wistfully sad that he had never been to the abbey. We followed him some way, when he stopped and asked if we were prepared to go by a rough route. On our answering in the affirmative, he led us over the white roads through olive groves, a short cut on the slopes of the hill to the right road up the valley to the abbey. On parting he showed himself to have been so pleased to help, he had quite enough time and seemed so perky as he rode off obviously to his afternoon's work, probably having come right out of his way.

The road to the abbey begins up the side of a stream for a while, then crosses and starts climbing steadily up the northern side of the valley, at first among olives and then small oak trees. Two or three summits became closer, dominant, when suddenly there is the view of Sassovivo built out on a promontory from the hillside, a perfect place of retreat, incredibly peaceful. It is now apparently used rather as a place of occasional retreat than as a full monastery, owned by a relatively new religious order. We studied the documents and notices describing the life of the Jesus Caritas Community, the "Little Brothers" who followed the memory of Charles de Foucauld, the missionary in the Sahara desert who died in 1916. During our visit we only just glimpsed a white-robed religious on the odd occasion but the atmosphere of the place certainly reflected their dedication as a community.

The special place of architectural importance and beauty is the cloister, well-preserved on all four sides, with series of round arches each supported on thin double columns, many of which were twisted into coils giving a delicacy seldom associated with Romanesque architecture. The cloister garth is paved all over, a slight slope rising to a well in the centre. When we arrived there was just one other couple, sitting by the well, reading. The setting gave an indication of the deep study and contemplation of the olden day Benedictine monks. Above the arches of the cloister was a marble frieze and above that on the church side a blind arcade in brick contrasting with the golden stone of the rest. There are even fragments of fourteenth century frescoes, including a Virgin and Child enthroned, just a remnant from its days as an active monastery.

Sassovivo cloister

We were able to wander round other parts of the monastery complex, down a great flight of stairs from the cloister, through a cobbled courtyard, into a number of halls and cellars, now used for meetings, and out into the gardens overlooking the valley. From here we looked up at the mountain peaks as the monks must have done, but probably then with a much greater sense of fear never quite knowing what marauders might invade their life. When we left Sassovivo we felt especially contented with a visit satisfying all our hopes, particularly knowing that it was not just a ruin but a place still used for much the same purposes as originally.

TREVI

S. Francesco, Trevi

More than any other Umbrian town we saw, Trevi belongs to the olive trees: every approach is through long stretches of olives, all views of the town set it among them. On our way up we came to the convent church of Madonna della Lacrime outside the town. It was shut, but we were able to go to the nunnery next door, were given by the nuns a key to the church and spent at least half an hour alone in the church, such a privilege. The "Epiphany" by Perugino is the highlight, a beautiful late work with a very light touch, in good condition on a side wall . This Renaissance church of the late fifteenth century with Baroque furnishings which for once were not overpowering, has many pleasant pictures and monuments. We were not rushed and were trusted to return the key when we had finished.

Above this, the road takes one round the old city walls all the time rising so that we entered by the gate above and to the south of the old city, on the spur adjoining the range of hills. We made our way straight to the pinacoteca which was adjoining the old Franciscan church; the gallery was newly built to fit alongside the old cloisters. When we were there it was not quite finished, although the pictures were perfectly housed and well displayed. There was nothing all that special, with work by Lo Spagna and Corraduccio possibly the best. The church, entered from the pinacoteca proper, was full of interesting items, particularly the early sixteenth century organ of local workmanship which is about to be restored, a piece of art work as well as a musical instrument.

Trevi

We continued our visit to Trevi by walking up into the old town where the duomo not only had its doors open at siesta time, but was open to the winds through at least two of its windows and part of the tower, causing an eerie clattering to accompany our visit. Restoration was much needed and indeed we wondered if parts would collapse before this happened. Some quite good fresco fragments remain after the Baroque development of the interior. Leaving the cathedral we wandered but the city was rather dark on a cold March day. The main impression was of great age, narrow streets and steps, the area around the duomo and the summit of the hill seemed set apart, a remnant from the past. The main public piazza and streets around it, well down towards the main entrance gateway, belonged to a slightly more modern world, the workplace of officials and traders. The real present was definitely outside that gateway near to which we were stopped by an artist standing at the doorway to his gallery studio. He seemed pleasant, very friendly even though we were clearly not to be customers; he sported an amazing number of artistic qualifications, but his work was not quite our taste of art. Nevertheless he was a good ambassador and enthusiast for Trevi, suggesting it would be a more glowing place in the summer weather.

Trevi

SPOLETO

Spoleto was at the end of a fairly long journey for us, but we made the trip twice to cover as many features as we could. The setting of the city, whether we arrived over the hills from the northwest or down the valley from the north east, was spectacular, on a hill below mountains on every side. At this time of year the mountains seemed threatening, certainly attracted any bad weather, more forbidding than most of the Umbrian hills we knew. Much of Spoleto being of a dark grey stone, there was a cold feeling even when the sun was shining. The contrast came with a warm or light relief in particular spots in and around the town, spots demanding a visit.

Spoleto

We were not really looking for Roman remains but Spoleto is so full of reminders of that age that we could scarcely ignore them. Near our first point of entry we found the Roman theatre, much of the bench seating rebuilt for modern theatrical use. At the opposite end off the city were the remains of an amphitheatre. In between, as we wandered through the streets we came on the dark and impressive Roman arch linked to the name of Drusus, appropriately it seemed summoning ideas of the dark episodes of Roman history still threatening Spoleto. As we often found later in our visit, Roman masonry appears in large quantities in many of the churches here. Possibly the most impressive remnants of these distant ages were those of the walls at the north west corner of what seems to have been the old Umbrian town, before the time of the Romans. Great blocks of stone hold up later walling high above the road below one of the preaching churches of the town, now deconsecrated and slowly being restored but for what purpose we remained ignorant.

We decided that the Cathedral would probably offer the best view of art as well as of architecture, at the start of our visit. The approach, unusually down hill, across a gradually widening piazza, is most impressive, possibly the most dramatic view of a Duomo in Umbria. The fine facade with Romanesque carving, eight rose windows and a thirteenth century mosaic, some of which was unfortunately behind scaffolding, is here enhanced rather than spoiled by the later addition of a Classical late fifteenth century portico across the width of the lower facade. It has a dignity giving a balance to the whole with on each side a very beautiful pulpit elaborately carved. On arrival, at about 11.40 am, we were pleased to see that the cathedral stayed open till one o'clock: so we could view it reasonably at leisure. No, this was not to be. Five minutes before noon a grumpy old man brandishing one big key, drove the visitors out. He was shutting at twelve: we showed him the notice on the door about closure at one, but he knew what he was doing and either could not or would not read. In fact, he was so quick that, if we had not protested, one lady visitor would have been shut in since she was in a chapel and had not been noticed. So our visit was cut short, one reason for coming back again, as we did a month later. We refused to let his episode turn us against Spoleto and immediately afterwards found a gentleman running a small card and gift shop, just above the cathedral, who in complete contrast never tried to rush us even though he also was expecting to close and we clearly were not a good commercial proposition.

Spoleto cathedral

The cathedral, as we really saw well on the second visit, is quite a treasure trove of art. The domed apse had been restored recently and is completely frescoed with four scenes from the Life of the Virgin, the last work of Filippo Lippi who died here at work in Spoleto. Quite how much was his work, or that of assistants or his son did not matter because the end result was very good: this east end was the finest of any church we found in use in Umbria. At the south west end of the nave two chapels can be found, the one leading out of the other, the first with a faded Pinturicchio fresco with a background we knew so well from our travels, that of Trasimeno. In the second chapel are less highly rated frescoes by the Sicilian Jacopo Santori who seems to have had quite a productive stay in Umbria. There were plenty of less important things to see including some fine sixteenth century wood panelling and a highly venerated icon in a special chapel, the image apparently deriving from eleventh century Byzantium, justifying all in all the hour we finally managed on our second visit, no grumpy old man in sight.

The duomo continued to show its complex character as we walked round the Rocca, built high above it. The east end, as we looked down to it, appears to be an incredible accumulation of buildings, showing no pattern at all, looking very little like church architecture as we expect it and providing a series of roofs all at different heights, various slopes and blocks, an accumulation of houses We chose this walk round for the views and at lunch time, the time of closures; we went on to see the medieval wall across the valley beyond. We were hardly prepared for the sight even though we had already seen it at a distance from below. Its height above the dry stream bed is particularly remarkable. This Ponte delle Torri, whether an aqueduct or a defence, is not only a prodigious piece of medieval engineering - one could hardly help but wonder how many men had died or been injured during its construction - but also a superb viewpoint from which to understand how Spoleto was the gateway on this road to the south. It almost seemed a fragile curtain now above a very dry gully thankfully not spoilt by the modern road which is tunnelled underneath the Rocca about here.

The remainder of our two visits to Spoleto was taken up with six churches, three inside the town and three outside the walls, four of the six being utterly different representations of the pre-Renaissance world of church architecture. Near the duomo is Sant' Eufemia, although we made this visit our final viewing of Spoleto. Yes, it has obviously been much restored and is no longer consecrated; there was a young custodian sitting at the receipt of custom by the door reading a novel and the hours of opening are somewhat limited. None of this affects the fact that this is perfect Romanesque, in a light warm stone, with patches of frescoes and a fully accessible women's gallery all round apart from the apse, affording views of the church not normally possible. Set in the courtyard also occupied by the Museo Diocesano, an old palace, it is a peaceful place whether for appreciating famous twelfth-century architecture or for just sampling a simple, well-restored medieval site, totally in contrast with the other two churches we visited in Spoleto itself.

San Domenico is one of the vast preaching halls so often erected by the friars, in this case given great character outside by the pink and white bands of the stonework. Inside an anonymous fifteenth century fresco of the Domenican saint Thomas Aquinas is well worth a look. Masonry work was being carried out at the west end where the facade promises to be good after restoration but is now causing noisy disturbance to the clerics running the church services as well as to visitors. The other church we visited could not have been more different. St. Andrew's is a Renaissance edifice of no special architectural or artistic importance. Instead, we were transported direct from the historical to present day religion at its most fervent. The church is now particularly dedicated to the memory, and clearly the active principles, of the newly beatified Father Pietro Bonilli who died in 1935. His presence was made alive by a great picture of the holy man at the nave end of the church with a good view of Spoleto painted in the background, giving us a modern version of what the much earlier visitors to churches in Umbria must have felt when confronted by a new fresco of Francis or Bernardino preaching.

Spoleto, San Pietro

In the outer area of Spoleto we found first the church of San Pietro set up on the lower slopes of the hillside across from the city. Inside, it is a horror story, of elaborate Baroque stucco draped and decorated with great curtains and friezes of faded red velvet. We quickly went outside again, for here on the nave front is a Romanesque picture gallery of sculpture from the twelfth century. The scenes are full of allegory and strange iconography but the depiction of both men and animals needs no detailed explanantion to make them instantly appreciable. The figures seems to stand out from the wall of the facade more dramatically than most such. It seems so sad that we cannot name this master of sculpture so that his name could be ranged along with the Pisanos and the masters of the Renaissance.

The next church to visit was San Salvatore, right over the other side of the Ponte delle Torri, north of Spoleto.

The way to and from where we parked was either by a roundabout pathway or through the cemetary. We chose the latter on the return journey giving us a very Italian experience. The mausolea, mostly in white marble, crowded the pathways, beautifully maintained often from at least the last century, mostly with flowers and plants clearly freshly brought and almost all sporting portraits, mostly photographs, of the more recently dead members of the family. It could easily seem macabre to visitors from northern Europe if it were not for the great richness of family life of which this is one aspect. This compares with the character of the family life where all generations live together, equally appreciated whether old or young.

Spoleto, San Salvatore

The church of San Salvatore was being restored; to be precise the west front was under wraps, while pieces of scaffolding and tools were visible inside. We learnt that Spoleto was a very important Dukedom in the seventh century and it seems that this church has really altered little from that date when monks from the east built it. Even then, it was sited here because there were early Christian catacombs nearby, and even earlier neolithic burials much where Spoleto's cemetary still is. The church has always been very close to the dead and its inside appearance retains a quality of suspension between the past and future death. The floor is better described as uneven ground with occasional paving stones. One wonders how the building has remained upright, it is such a mixture of Roman stone robbed from local buildings, crumbling columns, old apses and a totally chaotic mixture of architecture. The church leaves us with a sense of history and age hardly equalled elsewhere, as well as retaining, one way or another, some remarkably beautiful if decayed pieces of carving and fresco.

The church of San Ponziano, a quarter of a mile down the lane, is at first sight utterly different. The church itself is largely baroque and filled with the same awful red drapes as San Pietro. The facade is simple, set in a courtyard, now that of a convent of nuns who, we noticed across the wall, were trimming their vines and fruit trees: they quickly dipped away from view behind the wall as we were seen. We were lucky here not only to find the custodian but to find him very ready and happy to show us round, talking at length, full of history and illustrating his words with a formidable collection of picture postcards dating back sixty or seventy years. He soon led us to the crypt of the church, probably as old as the church of San Salvatore and using in its structure much Roman stonework including strange triangular columns said to have been used on the Roman race track. The frescoes here are well preserved, very old, of Byzantine character, again belonging to the time of the Dukedom of Spoleto. Our guide was full of anecdotes only some of which we understood through the barrier of language, giving us some insight into the so-called Dark Ages and treating Frederick Barbarossa as if he drove through here only yesterday. Clearly there are other views of history, glimpses through the buildings of the city, but at least we now knew that Spoleto, to some so well known for its modern music festivals, is also a treasure trove of the troubled history of ancient Umbria.

NARNI

Narni

We made the long journey to Narni late in our stay in Umbria, not very sure of what to expect and so we were considerably impressed by the position of the town rising up above a highly industrialised plain. Clearly there were some very old remains, walls clinging to the uneven promontory, but the interior of the old town seemed very irregular and rather muddled. The piazza supposedly one of the best in Umbria seems little more than a widening of the street surrounded by old buildings. Nevertheless Narni provided us with some interesting elements although we opted out from even attempting the very extensive underground city.

Walking across an unusual sloping triangular space, with the entry to a Roman cistern in the middle, we came to the Duomo of San Giovanali. A set of impressive steps led to just a side door while the main facade was crowded into a small street, a total contrast to Spoleto. Inside we were saddened to find restorers' curtaining around the best known details of the church, the early mosaics. Luckily, a lady who was a sacristan or verger, noticed us, came over and with enthusiasm showed us what were the outstanding parts of the duomo. By turning on lights, we were able to see the upper parts of the mosaics above the curtains and scaffolding. Clearly they will be magnificent. We were shown the two pulpits carved in the fifteenth century. Our self-appointed guide was most insistent on unlocking for us the plain crypt, taking us very quickly through and then on to her pride and joy, the surround of the high altar, an incredibly elaborate marble structure built on two levels, not exactly to our taste but impressive none the less: we tried to show our appreciation. More important for us was her ability to locate some attractive paintings by Vecchietto which we could easily have missed. Our memory here was of a rather muddled collection of interesting details and a very friendly guide.

Our wander through Narni took us next to the Piazza del Priori, whose main buildings, the Palazzi Comunale and del Priori, hardly stand back from the street. On the latter is another of the stone pulpits, a fine example of carving set up for herald announcer or denouncing preacher, while the former Palazzo shows on its front the fact that it is really an amalgamation of three towers. Here came a major disappointment, rather expected: in the halls of the palazzo the Ghirlandaio painting and the other art treasures were not to be seen due to restoration which may or may not have started but which certainly has no foreseeable end. Back in the piazza is a fountain dating from 1303, completing the ensemble of this ancient centre.

From here we moved on to the area of the ex-church of S. Domenico, visiting the garden of San Bernardo with its superb views down to the Nera river and across to the Abbazia di S. Cassiano, looking just as an abbey should, set in its trees on the slopes. Not being very interested in the underground old church of S. Domenico - which was just as well since it was firmly locked - we went on to the friars' barn of a church, deconsecrated and most extraordinary. It is now a library and centre for various local archives, where we were able to wander round with no-one among the quite considerable group studying in the library taking any notice. We looked at all sorts of sculptures of medieval and later time, various bits of unattributed frescoes and part of an environmental exhibition. It was as if we had stumbled into a museum most of whose exhibits were on site but not yet ready for viewing, still where they had been deposited while the curators had gone away for a year or two.

Since it was now lunchtime, everything else would be closed. After being kept amused by a class of primary children coping with greater or less success eating immense ices, we decided to move on from Narni, realizing that another visit in a future year might well enhance the good documentation we had gathered at the Tourist Office. Sadly, our attempt to get nearer to the abbey in the trees was frustrated, so we moved on to Amelia.

AMELIA

Amelia

With just a winter afternoon available we knew that we could only make a short acquaintance with Amelia. We were visiting for the impression of a medieval town rather than for any special buildings or art, and it was in the view of the place from about a kilometre away that we really gained the best picture the city could give us. It was built up from a wide base to a peak of a campanile. Our first close-up sighting was of the rather inappropriate late gateway set into the old walls and it was these which really impressed in many places round the base of the town, huge stones built up together as a mammoth dry-stone wall. The mind boggled at the thought of the mechanics involved in what was probably of pre-Roman time.

The climb up the town was through narrow old streets; we could guess that if seen from above, the roads and alleys would take on the appearance of a circular maze wandering around the hill. As we rose higher, stepped paths were alternatives to streets, the gardens became larger and more abundant and the view over the roofs expanded. The flattened summit contains pleasant palazzi and a great church, Romanesque with Baroque extras and beside it the piece de resistance, a tall, rough multi-sided campanile probably older than anything else in sight. Nothing particular to be seen and nothing open, we walked down as the traffic started to zoom back after siesta time bringing noise and rush to what had been very peaceful. Our drive out re-emphasised the cyclopean vastness of the wall blocks and the mount profile of Amelia from a short distance.

CARSULAI

Carsulae

Our return from the Narni area was punctuated by a visit, just off the main road, down a white track to Carsulai. We were not really chasing the remains of the ancient world but we could hardly miss the chance to visit this famous site. The setting was idyllic, green open spaces backed by strong curved hillsides. There were just enough couples walking around to remove the desolation and yet not to make it crowded. Here is a marvellous sense of space with considerable building remains: a beautiful contrast of white on green pleasing to aesthetic sensibility as well as providing an understanding of ancient habitation.

It feels very strange to walk along the stone roadway, Via Flaminia, which runs through the centre of Carsulai and now trails off north and south, giving the impression of being part of a still functional network and not just an isolated remnant. One arch has been re-erected, the steps up to one of the temples rise six feet or more, shop fronts are labelled, everything clearly explained on neat notices. At one point, a small chapel had been built out of Roman remains, presumably a little after the rest of the site was virtually abandoned. It is a rather pathetic, slightly out of place, addition to a site which is otherwise making no pretence, glorying in the fact that it is just scant ruins.

Two motorbikes race through the site on the white road and off among the olive trees: Carsulai relapses into silence and dreams. The mounds and foundations of the old theatre and tiny amphitheatre are peopled by ghosts of Roman times even in the present sunshine. The place must have been quite large; we can wander in any direction and still come across its remains. One could easily understand the eighteenth century classicists glorying in the romance of ruins, a remnant of Rome in the late afternoon sunshine of March, the wild flowers just beginning to take over and colour the green carpets.

CHAPTER 5

ITINERARY 5: Cerqueto, Monte Vibiano, Lagello, Cibottola, s. Apollinare, Agello, San Savino, Monte del Lago, Castel Rigone, Corciano, Perugia.

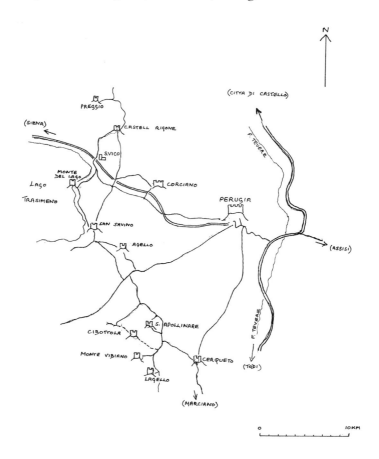

Map 5

CERQUETO

On many occasions we passed through Cerqueto on the way down to Marciano and the Tevere valley. One day we decided to investigate, in particular to go and find the parish church of S. Maria Maddalena. It was open and immediately we saw the fresco by Perugino of Saint Sebastian, with two other saints only just there at the sides probably the earliest dated work of his at least in Umbria. Though fragmented it was a beautiful example of the artist's skill in painting clothes and the moulding of legs. What was also interesting in this context was the reference on a plaque, outside a house nearby, that Perugino had come here from Perugia "scampato di pesta", not so much to paint here as to avoid the perennial problem of the plague.

Back inside the church were a number of other attractive frescoes, by the artist variously known as Tiberio d'Assisi, Diotelleve or even Tiberio Raniere d'Assisi, whose work we had especially admired in Montefalco. A full crucifixion fresco and fragments of a Madonna della Misericordia gave indications of what a feast of art had once been in this capella and was still here almost unnoticed. Finally, we saw a memorial to an Augustinian priest, still blessed and venerated in this church, a certain Giacomo Cinti of Cerqueto, who died in 1367. He was clearly still an important person in the twentieth century village.

MONTE VIBIANO VECCHIO

Mercatello

Monte Vibiano is approached through Mercatello, not much of a place it seemed to us except for two ancient remnants. On the way in, by the Nestore river, is a derelict mill: nothing very special except that this one has a machiolated tower as an integral part of it, conjuring up an unexpected vision of a member of a Robin Hood band, a fighting miller. Then, in Mercatello itself is a porticoed building clearly the market place of the place name, with impressive pillars surmounted by Corinthian-style capitals. The road then led steeply up past a modern church, steadily up the ridge-back towards the old village. Soon the route was lined by cypresses on both sides, of considerable height and age. The way into the village is dominated by the great platform holding a mighty palazzo, clearly very well restored and securely guarded, seeming to be within itself half the village and certainly taking up half the site on top of the hill. We learned later that this impressive place was owned by the head of the main bank of Perugia.

The rest of the village, a little old church, a dozen small well-kept cottages and a medieval gateway out of the other end, was almost predictable. No apparent life except a small parked car containing a sleeping and snoring man, who did not stir throughout our short visit. On this occasion we noticed that the white road passed on out of the gateway down, across and over the rolling hillsides towards an interesting-looking pile in the middle distance. Investigation was left to another day.

LAGELLO

Having seen Lagello from Monte Vibiano, we actually visited on another occasion and from the other direction, on one of our walks along white roads. We began from well below, in March, enjoying trying to identify the newly budding trees. We had by now identified Lagello by name, but we had little or no idea what it was but a number of cars passed us at the end of lunchtime, indicating a fair-sized village community. The buildings were often hidden from view as the road wandered until we arrived at an unexpected straight drive up, with neat parking places and shrubbery, and smart carved wooden signs headed "Borgo fortificato di Lagello". Large crowds must be expected of festive occasions. The drive then forked, one part through a private electrically-operated gate, the other now just for pedestrians taking us round to the front of the fortified walls, which formed more or less a square.

A gateway led in from a fine viewpoint on an open strand. Beside the gateway was a notice proudly proclaiming Europe Nostra Award, 1993, American Express Foundation. We wandered in to cobbled walkways between houses, steps up to doors, all beautifully restored with attractive plants in pots, almost deserted just now, except for an Italian radio program coming from an upstairs window. There were other normal signs of the inhabitants, children's bicycles and toys, cars and garden tools. It was saved from being twee, partly by the ochre-coloured stone which even in extreme restoration gave it a sense of strength. On one side the wall was missing, leading out to gardens, swimming pool and carpark. Possibly living here would include excessive restrictions on individuality or privacy, far from any shops, but for an outsider in the sun it gave a glimpse of a potentially idyllic place to live. As the notice said, 'Rispetate Silenzio', except for the radio.

MONTE LARGELLO

Lagello

CIBOTTOLA

CIBOTTOLA
CASTELLO

Cibottola castle

The little hamlet of Cibottola, high up on a ridge overlooking the Nestore river which winds its way from the north right round to the south of the hill, provided a point of identification for so much of the country around since its tower stands out for miles. Our way up was steep; after a few houses the white track took us for long walks on the ridge while the ancient hamlet sits on a bump along the ridge. A few houses, one large hidden palazzo in its trees, a bar and tables set out in a mini-park cluster round the old citadel. The place most alive was a farm just beyond with large numbers of cattle and horses which were dirty and unkempt shut up in sheds, farm machinery both very old and brand new, but no viable house: the farm workers lived down the hill.

We are told that St. Francis established one of his cells for friars here early on, from which it would have been possible to see across to Assisi. We certainly could see as

145

far but had no way of knowing whether the saint had actually been here: may be it was another case of the Queen Elizabeth slept here syndrome, but there was no doubt that the citadel was a place rooted in history as well as one of the best viewpoints possible. At some time the castle tower has been renovated; it is of an irregular heptagonal shape, effectively a prow of six sides looking out with the seventh longer one facing inside to the citadel. An entry arch remains, the old church and a sad-looking palazzo, now out of use and needing repair but occupying prime position. One can imagine that maybe in the eighteenth or nineteenth century quite wealthy owners once lived here, but then why did they live in such a remote place and how did their carriages make it up the hill. Answers to such questions remained uncertain and so gave the place its slightly mysterious charm, even if it was a sad one.

Cibottola view

We were told by some locals towards the end of our time in Umbria of an old convent building a little way out of Cibottola and we guessed that this may have had some

connection with that other tradition of St. Francis coming
to this village. Our route took us down what were strictly
private farm roads but the farmers themselves greeted us
in a friendly way and clearly no-one minded; we were
making for what was on the detailed map as Podere al
Convento, so clearly there had been a farm here since
the convent. A fascinating extra for us was that the local
farmer and his family had been working in the woods,
coppicing and thinning rather than cutting whole swathes
down. All the wood was cut to lengths of about a metre
and a half, and was now stacked by the side of the track
tidily about two metres high, with neat divisions about
every twenty metres along. What was particularly
impressive was that this stack stretched out for a full five
or six hundred metres beside the track. The family was
just packing up work for the day, mid-afternoon, as we
arrived at the old convent.

The buildings now showed up clearly in three parts, from
left to right, an ashlar towered section, a longer section
with few openings in local stone and fiinally a two-storey
house with loggia and cellars. The latter part was clearly
less old and was the remains of the farm house, occasional
parts of which had been used for animals quite recently.
The rest must be the old convent waiting for either total
disintegration or some sort of conservation or restoration.
At the moment though, it showed us how so many of
the buildings we had been looking at must have been
before restoration work this century and emphasised what
wonderful work had been done in so many places we
had visited. The mid-section of this Podere al Convento
was the old cloister, still mostly roofed with a ruinous

upper floor. On the walls were the disintegrating fragments of frescoes, probably not very old, weathered all over, often recognizably representations of the Madonna, angels or Franciscan monks. The paint was flaking off almost in front of us and the stippled plaster where the fresco was gone was itself coming off in small chunks. Were the half dozen logs and various bars of metal deposited there ready for use by restorers or were they just more of the dilapidated remains?

Podere al convento

The better stonework belonged to the old church, terribly overgrown with brambles and bushes but still entered by steps up from the cloister, apparently never from outside. The arches of many windows still stood and even in one part so did the vaulting. The highest walling belonged to the tower held up by the tendrils of creeper. The hillside around the old convent showed traces of old dry-stone walling, terraces and ancient remnants of olive trees while a little lower is a lake which could well have supplied the friars with fish. Much of the joy of the place was finding it right away from anywhere, and the fact that one could conjure up a complete way of life totally missing now but still to be sensed in what seem to be the true ghosts, the memories of past people and lives still lingering.

ST. APOLLINARE

St. Apollinare

A hamlet, a walk and some new views, we spent a number of sunshine hours in February as the first wild flowers began to appear beside the white roads. The first part of St Apollinare is one of the smallest walled villages possible, on a low spur above the Nestore river. On a late Sunday morning just dogs and cats welcomed us through the gateway arch into a tiny piazza with largely unrestored three-storeyed simple palazzi, one higher tower, then down a steep slope to the other little archway and out of the walls into farmland leading down to the river. The whole of it would have fitted into a small suburban cul-de-sac in Britain, yet was in miniature complete. There is a modern church outside together with a few newer houses. A gentle walk past these took us round through olive trees and banks of flowers up to the next spur where there was an older church, presumably originally belonging to what must have been a small monastery. Here, as we wandered, we encountered typical Sunday morning activity: a family party met up, greeted each other and parted in the courtyard outside the church, all in their Sunday best; a local man was taking for a walk a reluctant dog who much preferred to roll in the white road, while another small family group stopped their car and climbed among their olive trees, inspecting and looking for culinary delights on the slopes. All were very friendly to these strangers walking in on their lives. The church was open, simple but well-tended, with fragments of undistinguished frescoes and various signs of rebuilding over the centuries. We looked from it over the little river to the hillsides of Cibottola and other hamlets, and like the first butterflies emerging from hibernation, enjoyed the early glimpse of spring.

AGELLO

Seen from all around as we drove in different directions, Agello was impressive, well-built up on its individual hill, one of the largest villages crowning one of these nobbly protuberances so common in this area; almost all habitation seems to have been built high up in this part of Umbria. This village is now very much the modern living urban development, with many new houses, shops and a one-way system of streets to solve the problem of narrows and steeps. We walked up the last section and found a fascinating combination of new and old at the top. The largest building was a modern school, taking over the site of what could have been the old palazzo and fitting into its place remarkably well. It was nearly time for the end of the school day, and so a number of parents in cars were waiting, but none of them could get nearer than fifty yards because of the narrow approach while the two school buses had to wait at the bottom of a long flight of steps. For access, this must be one of the most inconvenient schools possible, but for views, one of the best.

Also occupying the summit of the hill where a Roman fort had been, was the remains of the medieval castle. The bailey-ward area had become a garden and belvedere, a view extending for miles in all directions. The old tower, still over a hundred feet high, showing the remains of shields of captains typical of a palazzo di podesta; it has been restored and is the centre point for the outdoor life of the village. Agello is a very good example of retaining enough of the old to give it a sense of history while being a fully active member of the twentieth century world.

SAN SAVINO

At the south east corner of Lago Trasimeno, San Savino occupies a small finger of hillside, pushing out towards the lake, its walls looking quietly impressive from the road which circles the lake. We visited one afternoon in February, not expecting too much but interested because we had passed it on a number of occasions. As we walked in, a delivery van was parked near the only gateway into the walled section and its driver reacted to the unexpected sight of two visitors wandering. He rummaged in the back of his van and produced with great pride a pamphlet of the Festa in San Savino of the previous August, of little meaning to us just now and full of local adverts. But it was the attitude of the man which was so good, so welcoming.

The design of the walls here must be very unusual, possibly partly the result of being built around some sort of convent, partly because of the site but particularly surely because of some enterprising architect of military defence. They form the plan of a boat, pointed at both ends and still complete to a two-storey height or more, with just the one gateway on one side. The only church is immediately outside this gateway. The archway leads into a tiny piazza, more like the entrance courtyard of an abbey, widening into a small square with an old central well. One street only leads off to a dead end, with old houses on both sides and room for gardens behind. The other end, the prow of the boat, is occupied by a triangular tower over twice the height of the surrounding walls. Could it have been the work of the same designer as that of Castiglione del Lago, or some unknown enterprising employee of the convent, resulting in a village, a fort, a religious community: it was hard to see which took precedence.

San Savino and Zucco

MONTE DEL LAGO

We visited Monte del Lago fairly late on a Febuary afternoon in not particularly good weather conditions, so that the pleasure we gained from about half an hour there is a good indication of the quality of this site. On a headland jutting out on the east of Lago Trasimeno, comparable with the now much larger Castiglione on the west, it is a small walled village around a central street which is really a set of shallow steps leading down to a bank above the lakeside. Beside the gate at the top was a fine machiolated tower as well as a spacious carpark commanding views over the lake and islands. On either side of the main passageway down, streets led off for twenty or thirty yards, coming to a stop at the walls Cars used all these ways treating the stepped sections as steps were made for vehicles to bump up and down. Much of the village has been restored, old doorways set beside plate glass windows, rough logs next to plastic fittings, cement mixers and yellow cranes still in use. Every few yards there was something medieval in origin, particularly a beautifully simple little chapel. The fact that our visit was in winter time obscured the probability that in the height of the summer the tourist use of the lakeside would spoil the peace of this village.

A little to the south of Monte, beside the road, was a romantic-looking ruined castle surround by curtain walls which seemed to include a small hamlet. It was in private ownership but as yet totally ruined, holes for windows, broken castellated towers and crumbling walls, with well-placed umbrella pines to give it character. The name Castell di Zucco told us little, leaving us with imaginative fascination; if only we knew something of its history, of the people for whom it was home and life, when it ceased to be a valid place to live, let alone, when it would become so again. Being so clearly fenced and wired in, we assumed that someone had plans for it and hoped that restoration would not spoil the romance.

CASTELL RIGONE

The hills around Castell Rigone north of Lago Trasimeno provided us with magnificent walks and our visits to the village seemed almost incidental. On the first occasion we climbed up from Magione by a series of hairpin bends arriving at a parking place next to a small hall proudly proclaimed on its outside as that of the Philharmonic Society of Castell Rigone. The way into the village was beside a small cafe, humble but providing us with one of the best coffees at a low price. The route led up steps to two small squares with tidy buildings around them. A number of restaurants were advertised but closed on this cool February day. The village was partly surrounded by walls including two towers, especially strong on the north with a sudden drop through trees to the valley below. The village was on a ridge which dropped down eastwards and then continued on and up beyond. Where it dropped, outside the line of the old walls, was a Renaissance church with facades in sandstone, a handsome building but since we were here in the early afternoon, it was closed. We knew little about it and were disappointed we could not get in, but soon more or less forgot about it, as we continued for a walk. We noticed just behind, a small chapel, older and now permanently closed and obviously disused, presumably the medieval predecessor.

S. Vico

Castell Rigone remained an area for lovely walks over the next weeks and we almost disregarded any study of its art or history. In fact, the image conjured up by the village was rather informed by evidence of summertime entertainment, including a large facility providing sports and activities as well as food. To the east, there was a new development of apartments, arranged in steps and coloured a vivid pink: we began to recognise this from twenty or more kilometers away as we walked different ridges. On one occasion on our way down from the Castell Rigone ridge following another set of hairpin bends directly to Lago Trasimeno, we found at the foot of the hill the tiny church of San Vito standing in an olive grove up a short track. Here was a small but remarkable campanile, clearly very old, its proportions emphasising its height because the square base was so small. It was in good but apparently unrestored condition. The little church beside it was closed. Later, in mid-March, we were driving through Castell Rigone after another magnificent walk and noticed the the Renaissance church's doors were open. We stopped and enjoyed a real treat, the more so because unexpected. The building is beautifully cared for, villagers came in and out renewing flowers and candles and there were informative leaflets in French, German, Spanish as well as in English. Despite the sad fact that the facade carving is suffering from the erosion of the grey sandstone and the fact that the campanile is a replacement of one that fell, this building lived up to the claim that it was the finest Renaissance church in northern Umbria. The carvings, especially those restored on the doorway of the western facade, are fine and complement the wheel-like circular window above: maybe the talk of the school of Michelangelo is fanciful, but the effect is of elegantly decorated strength. The inside, based on a Latin cross in plan, is enhanced by seven works of art at the appropriate altars, none of them great but all very remarkable and unexpected in a small village. Possibly the best is an Umbrian fresco of the Coronation of the Virgin by the artist G. B. Caporali, another link to Perugino; we liked this picture partly because its background seems just right for this temple on the hills above Lago Trasimeno.

Castel Rigone

We were glad to linger as the church was being made ready for a late afternoon service. The climax came as the deep bell of the campanile sounded out, a friendly old man from the village having come especially to toll it. We then continued our trip, driving on past the new development and over hills with superb views, now across the Upper Tiber valley, now back towards Trasimeno. Our destination was a tiny hill village, Preggio, to which the road eventually circled: we arrived in an open trangular piazza. Here, a service was in progress in the church, some villagers were starting the evening stroll and others were talking on the bench. There was little or nothing of art or great architecture, just a peaceful Italian village with its mixture of new and old. A short walk up from the piazza past two restored Renaissance houses took us to the remains of the medieval Rocca. The walls which must have formed a remote fortress then, now resisted our attempts to make much of its plan or appearance as a castle. From beside the walls the view down included, fifty feet below, a platform levelled out of the hillside, an all-weather football pitch and four or five teenagers reliving the escapades of their heroes from television. All ages were represented in this tiny out-of-the-way place.

CORCIANO

Half between Lago Trasimeno and Perugia, up above the superstrada, Corciano seems a proud place and justly so. Parking the car just outside the town walls provided us with the almost obligatory vista, but on this occasion the weather made it yet more spectacular. On the way there it was, and had been for some hours, raining heavily, but breaks were now appearing and the sun shone a moment producing one of the strongest and most brilliant rainbows we could remember, appearing to land only a hundred metres ahead of us. For the whole duration of our walk round Corciano the rain just held off, while dark clouds around re-emphasised the mass of the hills in all directions. As so often at such times, the colours deep and vivid. It was quiet this Saturday afternoon, but the young lady in the little tourist office responded to our inquiries with enthusiasm even though, I think, her office strictly was shut. This attitude seemed to pervade the whole town: they really were proud of it and it showed. Almost all the buildings were well restored and at numerous points all round were very attractive plaques giving names and details of buildings and famous sons of the place.

Corciano

The main entrance, up many gently sloping steps was through a machicolated gateway next to a great round and similarly fortified tower. Outside, a first world war field gun had been kept as a curiosity. Just inside was the main parish church; open, it contained two paintings of interest to us: a Perugino Assumption of the Virgin above the altar, an attractive picture in a grand frame and secondly a gonfalone attributed to Benedetto Bonfigli, an artist of the generation before Perugino, very much of this locality and who had come to our notice in the special exhibition of his works put on by the Art Gallery in Perugia. This, a Virgin Misericordia, was the only one of his works, if indeed it was, that we came across outside the special exhibition.

The rest of our visit was taken up with a wander around the streets, viewing good if not spectacular buildings, the palazzo del capitano del populo with three pairs of arches tidily arranged above each other, a smaller palazzo dei priori, a medieval well and church facades, all in the white and pink-tinged stone familiar from Assisi. There were proud references to their own cardinal, Luigi Rotelli of last century, and to the birth place of Corciano's own artist, Dona Doni, of the Perugino era. Clearly his family played its part in the history of the place as the plaque related. It told us that he was one of four brothers, the others a lawyer, a man of letters and a captain of men.

Pieve del Vescovo

Our way from Corciano by another road to the north of the town brought us to an edifice, in ruins, which gave us food for thought until eventually we pieced together what it was. On the map it was referred to as Pieve del Vescovo and, unused to this use of Pieve, it took us a moment to identify this as a bishop's palace. Standing on a low headland, it was a large square walled enclosure of three or four storeys with a courtyard inside (we could not get in) and on the front later wing pavilions added together with what must have been at one time an impressive entrance some two hundred years ago. All was now in ruinous condition, but there remained telephone wire attachments, slightly old fashioned but surely not more that fifty years old. On the far side were fairly modern out-houses and possible servants' quarters, sordidly disintegrating. Once this must have been a fine country residence, presumably of the bishop, or archbishop, of Perugia. Now it was rather disturbing relic, without the romance of a medieval ruin, inducing thoughts of why and when it had come to some calamity. We guessed that the time of the Second World War could probably be identified with its demise. Now, the road to it leads off to the side to a new business centre, suggesting the palace of the religion of the new computer age.

PERUGIA

Perugia

Perugia was the subject of a number of visits and still we only really came to know a part of it. From the first we experienced the main characteristic of the city, the wind, mostly cold, sweeping through the streets whatever its direction, most often straight from the snow-topped mountains on the horizon. Even when sunny, Perugia was windy except for a few favoured spots, on the steps below the cathedral in the sun or some sheltered garden. Our approach to the city was the same each time, because having been warned of difficulties we stuck to the route we found first time. Parking below the Rocca hill at the Piazza dei Partigiani, we always went up and came back down the escalators. Even when they became familiar these did not cease to excite and fascinate. We were going up or down as in the London Underground, the fixed stare of the passengers was the same, the same occasional notice or advert, there was piped pop music but the distances covered were much longer and instead of London's tight tunnel walls, there were holes, shadows and caverns, arches or pillars, sections of ruinous rock or rocky ruins and views ending in dim darkness which seemed to beckon one on for an endless following of Ariadne's thread. Surely there must be some Minotaur at the end. The reaction became more intense as we heard of the bloody and destructive history of Perugian family feuds, Papal tyrants and republican fervents leaving their mark here. And after all this we emerge not just into the daylight of the top of Perugia but at the end of that magnificent sweep of the great street, the Corso Vannucci.

Perugia, Corso Vannucci

I do not think we could ever stop enjoying this marvellous street, with the buildings becoming more impressive and genuinely old as we walk along it, the Perugian people, university students from all over the world and later, visitors; all spring there were top coats and fur coats draped, parading up and down, the world wandering and talking, showing itself off to everyone else who is returning their favours. True, in April the Corso was much more welcoming than in January and the pace of the people that much slower; the numbers were greater. But even in January all these characteristics were present. Our appreciation of the street was dulled just a little since the great fountain at the end was under a perspex half-globe for restoration work. The advantage of this particular form of covering was that we could see the work being done and even make out some of the Pisano carving; but from halfway down the street the dome still looked as if an alien spaceship had landed.

On our first visit to Perugia we found in the Palazzo dei Priori on the Corso Vannucci, the National Gallery of Umbria. This became a repeated port of call every time we returned to the city. Not only has it a very fine selection of local paintings and a smattering of some of Italy's best, the gallery itself has recently been re-constructed in the Palazzo so that there is never any sense of the crowding of pictures while there were large numbers of informative notices and computer information points, much of it in English. Also, for us, as ultrasessantenni, entry was free: more valuably still it was open throughout lunchtime, a real bonus. If it were not for this gallery and its special exhibition that year we would not have become so interested in Bonfigli, a predecessor of Perugino here in Perugia. This special exhibition helped us to appreciate that while Umbria or Perugia itself could never rival Tuscany and Florence, the art of the fifteenth century here was significantly alive, locked into the religious life, including fine architectural backgrounds from the Gothic city and well worth appreciative study.

Other places on the Corso Vannucci were not quite so easy to visit. The cathedral was closed the first time and when we did get in was a little disappointing because the inside was full of false marbling on pillars and walls. In compensation, we found a building that, more than most in our experience, really felt like a functioning cathedral rather than a museum. The Signorelli picture which the guidebooks placed in the cathedral museum had recently been restored and was now here in a side chapel. By the time of our later visits, the beautiful carved pulpit facing down the steps outside the duomo was out of wraps just newly restored. Not only was the Collegio di Cambio closed on our first visit in January, it was closed for restoration all the next two months, all the time threatening to be open later. Our persistance if not patience was rewarded finally in April, and as a bonus not only was the wonderful Perugino room fully restored, so was the inner room by later artists; and for some unknown reason our visit was free. It really was worth the wait, a magnificent feast of fifteenth century art.

Early on, in January, we walked down the Via dei Priori, past many dark old buildings and towers to the Oratoria di San Bernardino and the Franciscan church. Unfortunately the facade of the former was hidden from view as it was being restored while the latter is in ruins, with notices of promises to rebuild or restore it sometime. It was a significant reminder of the local destructive power of earthquakes and one wonders on the likelihood, even the wisdom of restoration given the history of this church for falling down in earth tremors. No wonder that the National Gallery up the road has so many pictures and frescoes that had once been in this Franciscan church. As a bonus, we found on the route back the small chapel of the Madonna della Luci, a little gem with a beautiful altarpiece by Caporali, follower of Perugino.

Another walk in the city took us from the Cathedral down the Via Rocchi to the fine palazzo which now houses the University 'per Stranieri'. Nearby is the most impressive gateway of the city, Arco di Augusto, which demonstrates in its ancient stone both the Etruscan and the Roman life of Perugia. From here we walked up the stepped street beside and above the walls. This route gave us views over to the snow-topped hills beyond the Tevere valley as we had a bird's eye sight of the extended walls round two finger-like promontories; these views were useful excuses to stop on the climb up the steps. One great lump of hill in the middle distance dominated the view, like a sort of loyal attendant, always there to show the mood of the day, snowy, dark or light with sunshine. This route brought us back up to two very different sites both of which we visited under the same ticket.

The chapel at the church of San Severo boasts the one work of Raphael definitely to be found in Umbria, although we found a few minor rival claims while this fresco is only partly by Raphael having been finished by Perugino: the master completing the work of his brilliant pupil. The chapel is hardly even an antechamber in size while the church and the rest of the monastery remain firmly closed and nothing to do with it. Here an attendant sits, hugging a fire when we visited, almost touching the visitors viewing the fresco on one wall of this cube.

Certainly the fresco is interesting although the Raphael part has suffered much damage, but the setting spoils the effect. While it was good to get near to the artwork as one would in a gallery, this cube room was a mess. While it is certainly very good to find art in its original setting, this place just did not feel like the original holy place with fresco but was just a mean commercial trap leaving a feeling that could hardly become a good memory.

Rather different was the impression made by the Etruscan Well. Down a little alleyway and through a dark museum entrance we walked into the top of the well on our own and straight into an amazing world of ancient engineering architecture. We could walk down steps to an arch spanning the great well hole, all dripping wet and echoing, so much larger and deeper than any ordinary well we might expect. Even to us, not especially conversant in the Etruscan story nor following any Etruscan or Roman trail, it was enough to conjure up the amazing skills of the ancient world and to realize how little progress was made over the succeeding centuries, as well as conjuring up an entrance to the Hades world of the underground.

Perugia, Sant' Ercolano

The street parallel to the great Corso Vannucci, Via Baglione not only reminds us by name of the bloody feuds of the medieval city but also has some fine buildings with late medieval facades and pulpit balconies. Leading from it, on another occasion, we made our way to Sant'Ercolano and the Porta Marzia. Here again the great Etruscan wall blocks are in evidence, the street of steps, the steps and facades of the octagonal church together make a fine ensemble looking back up to Perugia. Sadly the church seems seldom if ever to be open, but our way was along Corso Cavour to the churches of S. Domenico and S. Pietro, which between them give a distinctive character to the skyline of Perugia as seen from almost all directions, both campanile towers more outstanding than anything else in the city.

Perugia, San Domenico

The church of S. Domenico was, on our visit, an immense windy barn, doors at the end and on the sides all open. This was unfortunate because it was a cold day but in any case the main treasures of the church seem to be in the National Gallery. There were a few things to see apart from a plaque commemorating the city artist we had come to admire in the Gallery, Bonfigli, who was buried here. We were better pleased to go off into the cloisters of the Dominican convent, large and restored, leading to a big archaeological museum, and like so many cloisters a place of peace and quiet. We could also admire the colossal campanile of the church, Romanesque architecture moving into the realm of skyscraper.

Further down the road we came to San Pietro where we found not one but three cloister courtyards as we walked round the recommended tour into the garden organized by the Botanical Department of the University which now occupies the old monastic site; we finish our tour at the church. This garden was almost new, in its infancy in many parts although the basic trees have obviously been here for years. It is set out not just as a medieval garden and herbiary, but also illustrating medieval mythology. There is a simple water section set out to represent the Garden of Eden, a dark wood of the wild medieval imagery and an immense herb area referring not only to healing properties but also to supposed astrological qualities of the plants all set out in geometrical patterns. All this and much more is in the setting of the old entrance to the monastery, just inside the extended city walls, with clear labels explaining every little significance. A charming additional touch to our visit was a friendly and unexpected greeting from one of the students as she walked through, she being the weekend waitress at our local pizzeria. At one side the low garden wall gave onto a superb view towards Assisi.

Back in the monastery, the church of San Pietro certainly fulfilled the claim made, that it is the most interesting and beautiful interior in Perugia. The Romanesque pillars of the basilica hall, the vaulted aisles and gothic apse surmounted by a great coffered ceiling make it seem more reminiscent of the great churches of Rome, than typically of Umbria. Highly decorated throughout, there are many pictures of interest and value in the aisles and side chapels including a good addition to our collection on the Perugino trail. In the apse is a superb set of choir stalls carved in the early sixteenth century, inlaid marquetry, as also on the reading desk: we specially noticed a superb Annunciation scene. As if all this were not enough, we were lucky that the sacristan had opened up the sacristy and she was full of information about the art treasures in this further fifteenth century room. Small pictures from Perugino, Caravaggio and Parmigianino were to be seen, as well as a possible miniature Raphael, of the Two Holy Children, Christ and John the Baptist. The whole visit to San Pietro, at some distance from the centre of Perugia, was a culmination of many hours in this vibrant city.

Perugia, San Pietro

CHAPTER 6

ITINERARY 6: Citta di Castello, Montone, Pierli, Monterchi, Citerna, Sansepolcro, the 'Piero trail' (Urbino, Arezzo), Gubbio

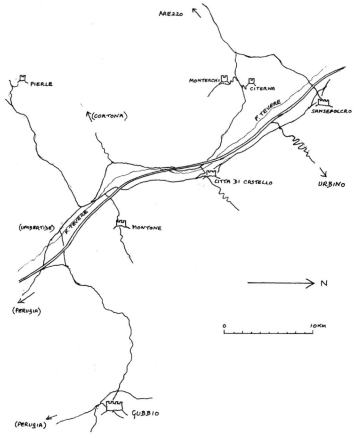

Map 6

CITTA DI CASTELLO

We arrived at Citta di Castello late on a Saturday morning in February, planning our museum visits for the afternoon. As expected, we found in the centre the Saturday market, just packing up and this gave us a theatre of entertainment: it was the first time we had really noticed the market vans with their awnings attached to the roofs. We watched one in particular as the stall holder put away the awning using a remote control. We were not the only audience, the young tradesmen had a number of female admirers watching. He cannot have had the mechanism all that long since he was not yet perfectly adept with the remote control so that the folding and refolding took some time and a number of abortive efforts. The end result was very neat removal away in a box. The clearing away was so much neater than at our local market in Britain, even though the immediate aftermath was just the same, mounds and scatters of rubbish. Here, the mechanical and human sweepers followed immediately on the end of the market and roads were soon washed and clean.

This modern activity enhanced the reality of the streets of old Citta: the market was centred on the Piazza Gabriotti, much of the old building around being in the dull, grey stone that crumbles and erodes all the time. The Palazzo del Comune has a tidy medieval facade and abuts onto the cathedral with its contrasting Renaissance front above tiers of steps. A stretch of gardens on one side of the Piazza extends to the city walls, providing a meeting or resting place for visitors and locals. Opposite the Palazzo del Comune is one of the few remaining medieval tall towers, once a prison. Behind the Palazzo next to the east end of the cathedral is a very different and odd tower, round, thin and tall, a bell-tower in an unusual and primitive Romanesque style. Much repair work is necessary around the area of its base: indeed, much work needs to be done in the town as a whole; some was being done at the time of our visit, particularly by way of re-surfacing streets and squares so causing some difficulty even to the pedestrian.

Walking through to the main Piazza Matteotti with its fine palazzi, now banks and offices, we passed the church of San Francesco which has a large plaque on its wall advertising the loss of its Raphael painting. The Wedding of the Virgin by the master was once in this church and is now in a gallery in Milan, while the Adoration of the Shepherds by Signorelli has migrated to the National Gallery, London. But at least the handsome palazzi have not been shipped out, many of them being restored and making the town well worth the visit. But no wonder the church of San Francesco is seldom open.

Citta di Castello

Our first museum or gallery visit was to that attached to the Duomo, set out in a series of rooms around the old cloister square. It was empty of visitors, attended by a very pleasant girl who gave us all the information she could, quite a considerable amount. The contents may not be outstanding but the quiet walk around allowed us to appreciate in turn the Treasure of Canoscio, early Christian eucharistic utensils, some very simple early Umbrian art and some later paintings by followers of Raphael and Perugino. We often find it difficult to become that enthusiastic about gold and silver religious treasures, of which there seem so many throughout the world, but we particularly enjoyed seeing a beautiful Paliotto, a sort of plaque, chiselled and embossed in silver and gold, dating from the twelfth century. The pride and joy of the museum, given a special place at the end of a clear cloister walk, is the Pinturicchio Madonna and Child with John the Baptist, a strange mixture of primitive iconography, especially the prematurely old Christ Child, together with the delicately painted features of the other two faces, and of hands, finished with a background of feathery "Umbrian" trees.

The other place to visit this afternoon was the Pinacoteca, where the building was almost as good as the exhibits: a palace of the fifteenth and sixteenth centuries, belonging to the local and dominant family of Vitelli, with frescoes not only in the main rooms but also on the "garden" facade, the design of Vasari. The atmosphere was a little spoilt by the unusually grumpy ticket seller and custodian, encased in his desk surrounded by television screens of the various rooms. I do not think he really took much notice of those, let alone of the few visitors. We went to look at the facade first, backing as it does onto a wide space, now just rough grass but promised to be developed into an Italian garden: it was certainly very far from the cannon-foundry or deposit which had originally been here and had attached its name to the Palazzo. Inside, the staircase and many of the rooms retained restored frescoes, though all linked to Vasari as designer, the work of a multitude of less well-known artists of the sixteenth and succeeding centuries.

The specially noted exhibit of the gallery is a rare Umbrian Raphael, a bit of a non-event, because the Pala, or Standard, attributed to him is in such a fragmented state that the character of Raphael's work hardly showed on either side. It was a case of, "if only". On the other hand there was much else of quality, particularly a dramatic and unusually vertical representation of the martyrdom of St. Sebastian by Signorelli, with its characteristic ration of human anatomy so strongly painted. There were some more early Umbrian altarpieces and a large number of terrocottas belonging to the production-line of the Della Robbia family, attractive whether or not they were genuinely by one of the named brothers: did it really matter? We also had the chance to get to know, through a number of impressive large paintings, the work of Raffaellino del Colle, a local man of the generation following Raphael himself. As in the other museum of Citta, pride of place here belonged to goldsmiths' work: a beautiful reliquary dated to 1420, linked to Ghiberti, with two statuettes in particular of Saints Francis and Andrew in gold-plated silver, as good an example as we could ever expect to see.

MONTONE

Montone

We had been given a small leaflet for Montone on our visit to Citta di Castello, by which we knew that the small gallery would not be open - only on Saturdays and Sundays at this time of year; but the hill-town attracted us in itself, in an area new and rarely visited by us, off the upper Tevere Valley. After a steep climb up from the main road we found that the town was really built on two summits, the one monastic, the other feudal in origin, with a small town gate and piazza in the dip between the two. The stone lacked the pinkish tone of further south, Assisi or Spello, but had a bright fresh texture as if it had just been cleaned.

First, we climbed the summit with the San Francesco monastery on top, walking through a restored gothic gateway and up a steep set of steps towards the convent. This hill, while full of houses, mostly restored, was unlike many hill-towns since there were many bushes and gardens making their presence felt and not hidden out of sight. The monastery which now houses the gallery was at least open for viewing the cloisters, a clean pale yellow stucco outlined by bricks, an upper storey above the colonnades and surmounted in one corner by a brick tower. All was totally empty on this February morning and absolutely peaceful. Just through the walkway an arch led onto an extended platform to view the small tributary valley winding up into the wooded hills towards Gubbio.

There were a few people in the little piazza down between the hills: this was the first place in Montone where we noticed reference to the best-known historical figure of the town, Braccio Fortebraccio. Identified as the condottiere *par excellence*, he was something of a military genius and had a major impact on Umbria in the years around 1400 until his death in 1424. Most of the local hill-towns, as we had already seen, owed a part of their history to this "strong-armed" man who was clearly quite a politician as well. The names of piazza and buildings remind us of the time when Montone became the head of a significant county, until the papal states took over from Fortebraccio's son and heir and the town reverted to its minor role.

Montone tower

On the second summit of Montone the streets and houses were closer together and less restored, leading steeply to an open space beside another church and the remnants of a Rocca, the whole effect more typical of an Umbrian hill-town. We talked to a local who, as we found so often, was friendly, very proud of his home town and extremely voluble. We found that the image on the front of our guide pamphlet, of a restored castle, was in fact well away from Montone town, although it could be seen dominating views. This was a disappointment, since it would have fitted in so well up here. Instead, foundations at the top of the hill and a great hulk of a seminary barracks were all that there was to help us to imagine what it must have been like with castle and walls complete. We finished our tour by walking round the rampart road on the eastern side, where the village could so easily be falling down a crumbling hill. Substantial work had been completed in one part, providing a magnificent balustrade, while yet more work was in progress further down below us to make sure that this and all above it did not slide into the valley. The extent of this work and particularly the elaborate viewing platforms cantilevered out over the cliff amazed us.

PIERLE

PIERLE

Pierle from distance

The road which runs just south of Citta di Castello westwards, divides into two just before it crosses the hills to Trasimeno or Cortona, both roads giving on to magnificent views. We first saw the castle of Pierle as we climbed the southern of these two forks from Lisciano to Tuoro; the donjon castle flitted in and out of sunlight. On another occasion we took the other fork and investigated the tiny hamlet clustered below the ruins of the castle, all perched on a promontory of the hillside. On the upper edge of the hamlet is a small apsed Romanesque chapel, presumably built by the one-time owners of the castle. The cluster of houses, well-kept with attractive little gardens, seemed to take absolutely no notice of the great castle walls, while the people we saw were very friendly to these odd visitors staring up at the donjon.

Pierle tower

The castle is apparently completely unrestored which makes it more surprising that it has survived to such a height. From nearby it is almost impossible to see the central donjon, surrounded as it is by high curtain walling, even though the keep must still be six or seven storeys high. At the upper end is the remains, very overgrown, of a small sally-port, but otherwise from the tracks round the castle in the hamlet there is no entry at all. Right on the end of the promontory was originally a complicated barbican entrance, much of which seems to have fallen down the hillside so that hardly a path is left, all totally overgrown and full of brambles. Entry to the castle at present is totally impossible. Much the best understanding of what now remains can be gained by walking a little way up the hillside above the village, so that one can look down on the main outlines of the buildings. The site, the magnificence of castle building, the brooding power which still pervades the place makes one wonder about the history, the castellans or local barons who must have totally dominated the valley.

MONTERCHI

Monterchi

This day's trip was an important one in our following of the Piero della Francesco trail, which for us began in Perugia National Gallery, was then frustrated for the time being in Arezzo, and now made headway here and in Sansepolcro on the same day. Although we would probably never have thought of coming here to Monterchi, just in Tuscany, if it were not for the trail, the small town is an attractive one to visit.

We knew that the picture, the Madonna del Parto, had at one time been in a cemetary chapel but was no longer there, but we were not quite sure what to expect from the information which stated it was now lodged in an

181

ex-school. A most ordinary building hardly prepared us for the single-minded exhibition for which we paid our lira to a custodian who was intent on watering his plants outside. He directed us to four rooms in turn. The first, to which we could and did return at the end, was a bare room with just the Piero fresco on a piece of wall in it. Nothing detracted from the impact of the picture and we were lucky, at the end of February, to be there on our own and unrushed. Not only is the picture unique in subject matter, its composition is so perfectly balanced that one is mesmerised into a single vision, seldom true of so many works of art whose composition takes one's eyes on a journey round the picture. The other three rooms demonstrated the best of modern museum presentation. In the first, we were shown by multi-picture projection how the restoration of the fresco had been achieved - all this to a choral background from the village, on tape. In the second, the life and works of the artist on video were complemented by photographs around the room. In the third room, the restoration story of the frescoes in S. Francesco, Arezzo, was shown with diagrams, story and a mini-version mock-up of the sanctuary in the church. We could not decide whether this made up for our being unable to see the real thing in Arezzo a few days earlier or whether this was adding insult to injury. After a long inspection of each room, we returned to the fresco itself and completed a most unusual but very satisfying experience.

Was there anything else in Monterchi? We had no idea and to be honest found little really exciting, but it gently repaid half an hour's inspection. Inevitably it is set on a hill and has narrow and steep streets, including one with a real medieval "feel", too narrow even for Italian cars, taking the visitor through kennel-like arches. The big church at the top was locked, the old Medici fortress was little more than a platform and a tower, the piazza pleasant. The balcony part way up gave a wonderful view of the side valley here and down to the Tevere beyond. It was sunny and peaceful in a restored Italian village and we were suddenly brought back to earth and tragedy by a plaque on the side of the Piazza dedicated to three members of the Central Indian Horse, dated 23 July 1944, reference to two posthumous George Crosses (why two not three?), memorials to one Briton and two Indians who had died going to rescue a colleague in a minefield. We were often seeing references to Italian dead of both wars, of the resistance or abroad, but this was particularly poignant and pathetic. We wondered what the present Italian young made of it.

CITERNA

Citerna

A lunchtime interruption of the Piero trail between Montercchi and Sansepolcro led us up to the village of Citerna on the hill across from where we had just been, oddly back in Umbria rather than Tuscany. It looked interesting even if there was no special art or building to be seen. After a steep climb we parked alongside the old citadel walls, now forming houses. We noticed from below that one set of windows seemed to have no frames or glass but this meant nothing to us until we climbed a set of steps to the old town. Citerna now provided us with our first experience proper of a "caminamenta", the old covered walk following for about a hundred and fifty yards round the walls, below the present houses. One could imagine stalls being set up in the olden days at each stage of the walkway, lit by the open arches we had seen from below. At the end another set of steps led through a tunnel up to the main street; if we had just walked into the village by the medieval gateway and up the street, we would never have known of the existence of the "caminamenta".

The street bent into a small piazza farther up, with the main church which contained a number of quite impressive sixteenth century pictures; it then stretched further up to the old Rocca. The remains of the old fort had been renovated to contain very pleasant gardens. The one remaining curiosity we found was a brick round tower, out of place among the other stone fortifications while dotted across the whole area were a number of statues and carvings suggesting a Roman or earlier origin. It was a pleasant place to spend an hour or so at lunchtime.

SANSEPOLCRO

Most visitors only go to Sansepolcro for the art, in particular for the Piero della Francesca pictures, and otherwise would not make the trip. Although we found that the modern town is clearly industrial, the old elements suffered much in the Second World War and the whole area is flat, it is certainly not uninteresting.

The gallery of Sansepolcro, in Museo Civico, is entered from outside one of the gates, Porta di Castello, as if going back into the wall. The great masterpiece, "The Resurrection", everyone comes to see, originally painted in fresco for next door, is on the wall to which it was moved about a century later and now looks as if it was made for the room, a room that is now devoted solely to this painter, containing also his Polittico della Misericordia and two fresco fragments. Curiously the room has an external doorway filling most of the wall opposite to the 'Resurrection', leading on to a staircase to the street, the doorway now sealed with glass. The result is that not only does it seem to allow much more natural light into the room and on to the paintings than normally, but a glimpse of the painting can be gained from outside the Gallery, standing inside the walled town.

Little could be added to the many words written about this picture. Our reaction on seeing two of Piero's great frescoes in one day was that the 'Resurrection' is a very disturbing picture with none of the stability of the Montercchi Madonna. It does not really seem to belong to the same age, appears much more modern, the soldiers angular with disturbed postures even in sleep, the Christ figure almost stepping out of the picture at one, the background surreal. It is one of those pictures to stand, or preferably sit, and stare at, rather than be lectured about - comments can come later.

The other pictures in the room are worthy in their own right. The Polittico has a central Madonna calmly holding out her cloak to cover donors and worshippers. As so often, the predella pictures are miniatures, gems, complete entities on their own. The two fragments of fresco indicate how much is lost to us from the time of these great artists; in this case, the fragment of San Giuliano has all the wistfulness of a half-remembered dream.

Obviously, the rest of the museum is a bit of an anti-climax, but it has some fine pictures from both the early Renaissance and the later sixteenth century, all set out well. From the Museo Civico, the Piero trail took us a little way along the first street back inside the town to the Casa di Piero della Francesco, the reminder that the artist was himself of this place. A remarkably long and large Renaissance building, it had little sense of atmosphere for us, apparently perpetuating the image of Piero as one who would always remain intangible. A little further on we drifted into a guild chapel where restoration "blow-work" was going on disseminating dust all over the building, and us.

Sansepolcro

The town is full of interesting facades. The best of the towers is gone, a casualty of the war, but the main piazza, still named after it, has a wide open space and dignified buildings. The duomo has been rebuilt much but has a sense of strength inside and includes many works of art even if not firmly attributed to well-known artists; an early wooden crucifix was as crudely impressive as any we had seen. We also looked in a number of lesser churches and while licking a mammoth ice-cream admired the late town walls belonging to the same era as the Medicean fortress.

THE PIERO TRAIL

The last two stages of our trail after the work of Piero della Francesco were strictly outside Umbria and southern Tuscany. Because we completed this trail at the same time as the rest of our Umbrian escapade, here is reference to both other places where we found Piero's art.

187

In Urbino, we visited the Ducal Palace, far beyond anything to be found in Umbria, except possibly in Gubbio. The regulations of the visit were very ordered, we had to book the previous evening and even then were only just allowed to tag on the end of a large party visit instead of waiting hours for the next chance. It turned out to our benefit since we soon found ourselves slower than the rest, so that one of the two security guards allotted to the party stayed with us, and we could let the crowd go on ahead. We were never rushed and saw all the rooms and pictures, including the extraordinary and beautiful wood-carving of the study, in perfect peace and quiet.

When we reached the Piero pictures we both had something of a shock. I think we were expecting the Sinigallia Madonna to be quite small but for some reason were shattered by the size of the famous Flagellation, expecting something much larger: both pictures were so much smaller than his work in London National Gallery, for instance. Despite the size, possibly even partly because of it, both pictures were more enigmatic to us now, in real life as it were, than book illustrations. This was the highlight of a very short trip to Urbino, otherwise so important for the background of Raphael.

The frescoes in Arezzo were still being restored and on our first visit we could not get anywhere near to Piero's great cycle of the Finding of the True Cross. We had to be content with the little fragment in the Cathedral, together with much other beautiful architecture. Then we learned that it was possible, if we booked weeks in advance, to go up on the scaffolding and view the parts that had already been restored in the east end of the great Franciscan church. We duly booked for 9 am. on an April morning, well knowing that we would have to leave at six in the morning to get there early enough to register for the visit.

It was almost inevitable that when the morning came it was the coldest one of the spring months and there was a deep frost. On the way to Arezzo once we had cleared the car windows, we came across every possible obstacle we could imagine, school-buses stopping, tractors on the way to work, roadworks including cement-mixing lorries delivering their contents, broken-down vehicles and of course every red light working against us. We were so nearly late that parking became a problem to the extent that some Italian bureaucrat is still probably trying to work out how to fine us. We almost ran to the church, arriving to put on our regulation hard hats and climb the scaffolding ladders with a select group of Italians, commentary all in Italian, to see at a distance of little more than an arm's length the whole of one side of the choir, frescoes of episodes from the legend of the finding of the True Cross. Even when all restoration is finished, we would never be able to see the upper ranks of these frescoes so wonderfully, while on the other side we could watch the experts working, everything linked to a series of computers as in a high-tech scientific laboratory. We could have stayed there for hours just drinking in the art and the experience, but the visiting time was sadly limited: at least we had completed this Piero della Francesco trail in a manner which we would never forget.

GUBBIO

Gubbio

On a Sunday after about thirty-six hours of rain, we made the journey over hills each marked by its regulation set of cypresses, to Gubbio. It was cold and Gubbio was all height: the town rose from its base near the church of San Francesco to the high point of the Duomo, the Palazzo del Consoli was itself such a high building even when seen from right down below, the town walls circled even higher up the mountain and far above them at the end of the *funivia* was the tiny image of the church of San Ubaldo on the top of Monte Ingino. The cold weather, the snow on the peaks behind Gubbio, all this height of the town, we felt we had moved into a new part of Umbria far away from the gentle regions of Perugia and Trasimeno. The next time we saw it in gentler weather.

On both our visits we climbed up to the Duomo, past other places to visit, then right down again at lunchtime and back up again to the Palazzo del Consoli. Crazy maybe, but the purpose was to fit into the possible opening times, much as it was also one way of trying to keep warm in February and of getting fit. All the streets, many of which were simply sets of steps, channelled the cold air even if there was little wind. The dark stone of most of the buildings, so different from Assisi, was equally cold, while the stream rushed down from snows above, through stone channels, under several bridges and always around the corner across the lower part of the town. This was no time for looking and staring at facades and imbibing details of architecture, much as we would have liked.

The exception was at the Piazza della Signoria, the one open space in full sunshine where we were able to indulge the pleasure of standing and staring. The terracotta-coloured paving of the piazza, one side an undistinguished street, another a small and quite plain medieval Palazzo Pretorio, the third side a balcony wall, the piazza had one purpose only, the frontispiece for the Palazzo del Consoli, deep enough to balance the height of the Palazzo: it was a meeting place for all in their Sunday best, long coats and furs, before lunch on our first visit, but then almost empty late in the mid-afternoon. Though the cold funnelled down all the streets, here it dissipated making the piazza the warmest spot in Gubbio. The view from the balcony was as spectacular as we could expect, although the wall is just too high for convenient viewing - at the same time, safe, I suppose!

Gubbio, Palazzo del Consoli

We began by visiting the Palazzo Ducale of the Montefeltro era, high up in the town cheek-by-jowl with the west end of the Duomo. The courtyard, immediately inside the entrance and free to view, is beautiful early Renaissance elegance especially attractive because of the grey pillars and the pink walling complementing each other. Sadly the pillars are of the stone we were so often finding worn away by erosion so that the carving of the capitals was scarcely there. The palace now houses a small gallery, where the contents are of less interest than the restoration of the ducal rooms. There is no great medieval or Renaissance art in Gubbio, except for the buildings themselves. Here, we were not ourselves particularly interested in the finer points of the impressive archaeological discoveries made in the lower part of the Palace. More valuable was the chance to go up stairs to the first floor of the courtyard and view each facade from above. People had been packing up modern sculptures from a recent exhibition, leaving for the moment an odd mixture of all sizes of packing case, various statues and notices.

The Duomo is a fine mainly Romanesque building, built incredibly close to the Ducal palace almost as though the dukes must supervise everything that went on in the cathedral; neither palace nor duomo had any space to show off an external facade. The north side is built so closely into the side of the hill that no windows were possible. The building is a great hall whose roof is built up by a series of some eight great arches like the up-turned ribs of a boat, giving a tunnel effect: these pillar ribs give the impression that the walls of the building lean inwards. There are no great or memorable treasures here, but all round were tasteful pictures and carvings, very little inappropriate Baroque over-indulgence. Monuments such as the stone image of a bishop on the floor help to make it more comparable to a northern cathedral than the usual Italian model. One of these monuments is strangely built into the west wall, high up both inside and out: clearly the Gabrielli family not only provided bishops for Gubbio, but also contributed to all aspects of medieval life.

Instead of going back down into the town immediately, we walked up above the cathedral towards the highest gate of the city. The old walls wander up and down the slopes like stone caterpillars raising their heads at the towers. The land here is so steep, could there ever have been houses to be protected or was it always vegetable patch and pasture? It is coming up to the Italian off-period, lunch time, and especially on Sunday everyone disappears off the streets. It is too cold to sit around and although the sun is shining that makes no difference in so many of the streets that go across the hillside. They always seem to be in the shade. At this time of year almost all the cafe-bars are shut; when we return in March, they are nearly all open for the first trickle of tourists, but now we are hardly expected to be here.

On the way down from the cathedral we pass again the famous wine barrel behind an iron grating across a doorway incongruously small compared with the barrel. Down steps, never moving in a straight line for more than a few yards, we find a dark square, bleak in the winter, faced by the Palazzo del Bargello, medieval, grey and forbidding. In front of it is the Fontana dei Matti, equally old and grey: we are told that if we walk around it three times we go mad and that this is how it gained its name. We would be mad to do so since it is so cold just here, whatever the legend. Soon, we cross the stream rushing down the hill reminding us how close the Italian towns are to the elements. After several Renaissance palazzi we find ourselves almost where we started, near the Logge dei Tiratori, the restored brick wool-drying sheds and the square which commemorates heroes of the Resistance. Down here we find a coffee in a little bar which shows us another side of the family Sunday lunch. Two youngish women are ready to serve, hardly looking at the television playing away in the corner, obviously bored as can be. Quite good coffee, but then . . . enters a barrel almost as big as the one behind the grill, greasy long hair, leaning on the bar, trying to be familiar, wandering off to make a 'phone call, flicking bits of paper around. It could be a back street joint anywhere in the world, so even Gubbio on a Sunday can come to this.

We continue our visit by looking at two churches, S. Francesco down here and S. Giovanni a little way up again. The Franciscan church is typically large, had late frescoes in many parts and is the venue this Sunday for a service emphasising the place of the disabled in God's Kingdom, the bishop all in white celebrating mass. S. Giovanni has a good Romanesque facade with campanile attached, while inside is an attractive fresco of the Madonna and Child with musicians by Raffaellino del Colle, whose work we found particularly in Citta di Castello. We do not need to linger because the Palazzo dei Consoli will now be open and we can come to the climax of our visit to Gubbio.

Gobbio, Palazzo gallery

The fact that it is free to older citizens of the "European Union" is immediately attractive: in fact we find the museum or gallery itself would not really be worth all that money. The hall immediately inside is as great and magnificent a structure as any medieval baronial hall we have seen, at least half the whole height of the palazzo, with a stone staircase at one end providing a gradually ascending view right up to the stone vault. This way up is much more attractive than the secret passage of steps that is an alternative, giving a dramatic view down the hall almost from roof height. In a room accessed from part way up the stairs is the special curiosity, Gubbio's "Rosetta stone", that is a set of seven copper plates known as the Eugubine Tablets. Found in late medieval times by a shepherd, they have writing both left to right and right to left; of clear value especially to scholars studying the old languages; we look, are impressed and pass on, suitably aware of having seen something special. Upstairs is the picture gallery, nothing very special, a collection of old local medieval altarpieces blended with seventeenth and nineteenth century local artist's work. The setting of the old rooms is pleasant although we felt a bit concerned for the guardian, heavily coated and still shivering over his gas stove. The real treat was still in store for us.

Through a passage from the gallery we could go out to the great stone loggia high up on the face of the palazzo overlooking the town. The sun shone in at one corner, we could view in any of three directions and did not have to rush, there was hardly anyone about. The view is exceptional. We looked down to the great paved piazza in front of the palazzo and then over sets of roofs down to the wool-drying sheds and S. Francesco. We could see the circles and arches of the Roman amphitheatre beyond, the midget cars on the roads leading across Italy and the great cement factory to the north, old and new all mixed across the landscape. Beyond the valley were the hills between us and the Tevere, over which we had driven and from which we had witnessed the special first dramatic sight of Gubbio. And to the south, out of the side corner of the loggia, we could look not only at the church of S. Ubaldo on the hill behind and the chair lift making its way up, but also this February day, to the snow tops of ranges of peaks in the Umbrian hinterland. This was certainly worth the climb, the loggia would have been worth the fee we did not have to pay. In two visits to Gubbio, the chance to stop and stare with such a panorama from a spot made so long ago was the highlight on both occasions.

Gubbio

CHAPTER 7

ITINERARY 7: Chiusi, Cetona, Sarteano, Monte-
pulciano, Pienza, Spedaletto, Monticchiello, S. Anna in
Camprena, Petroio, Cennano, Monte Olivetto Maggiore,
S. Quirico d'Orcia, Bagno Vignone, Castiglione d'Orcia,
Rocca d'Orcia, Montalcino, Sant' Antimo, San Galgano.

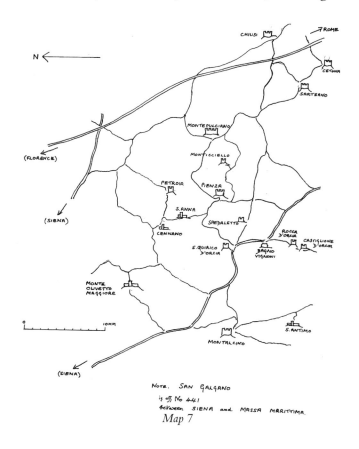

Map 7

CHIUSI

Chiusi

We did not go to Chiusi to see Etruscan remains, we were not really so interested in them. For those who are, this was obviously a town which must be visited, but we arrived early one morning by the accident of delivering travellers for Rome to the station. The main street of the old town was half out of action, being dug up. Our slight disinterest on a cool morning was quickened by the very helpful lady in the Tourist Office, one of the most friendly, but as we found out even she could not do anything about the fact that the cathedral museum was firmly closed even though supposed to be open; so this was one place we missed seeing. The cathedral itself was strange. Parts are and seemed to be old, but so much rebuilding and refurbishing has taken place that architecturally it is a muddle. At the same time the end result is harmonious and the mosaics of late last century fit in well, giving the building a slightly exotic look.

After a walk round the town where we came across old Roman or Etruscan stones at every other corner, we took ourselves almost against our better judgement to the Etruscan museum. The visit started well because we got in free! Both of us were unexpectedly pleased by the exhibition, very full of artifacts well-presented on two floors with good modern explanatory material. In particular, we spent quite a time looking at the carvings on the Etruscan funerary lids with their portraits of both male and female honoured ones, together with pictures in stone of everyday life. Some of the votive figures in bronze reminded us of the Giacometti figures recently exhibited in London. For the Etruscan buff this museum and the whole local area must be quite wonderful; for us ordinary mortals the museum was a revelation.

CETONA

Cetona

Aside from providing us with a very good restaurant at lunchtime, with delicious local fare, Cetona felt very different from most of the towns of Umbria and southern Tuscany. The start of our visit was in a big broad piazza, more like one of the best English market-town high streets, with the old hill town on one side. The buildings were mostly not very old by Italian standards but all were dignified and looked warm in the sun. We found that the Rocca was in private ownership, without any large tower but with an elaborate staircase with access to the top, now behind locked gates. The streets all go round the lower stages of the Rocca, but seldom did we feel constricted in them.

The special joy we found in Cetona was the continual but changing views as we progressed especially when we reached the higher levels where a path replaced the road, looking down over the gardens of the layer below. To the west the slopes of hills, covered with trees of all sorts, mounted to the impressive summit, Monte Cetona, with wireless mast on top of its pimple. To the east the vistas opened up across the wide Chiana valley to the hills of Umbria. On our way round we found the Chiesa of the Holy Trinity, with a small piazza formed by a sloping platform in front of the facade, all parallel with the road round. In the church were some fifteenth century local frescoes and rather unexpectedly across here in Tuscany a sixteenth century Umbrian 'Coronation of the Madonna', a useful reminder that the border between the two provinces is no hard and fast one. At one point on our walk, where seats were conveniently placed beside the path for us to sit and stare, the old wall mounted up the side of what was here a very steep slope, rising in steps and mini-towers, as if this was a private way in or out for the castellan without having to touch the town itself. Our visit was rounded off by a typical motorized incident to watch. The old man had parked his three-wheel van up at the corner of the house. He was about to drive out so he just let off the breaks and the van fell back round the corner until it hit the house wall opposite. Quite unconcerned, the driver now started the engine and drove away, the little "lawn-mower" engine tootling up the narrow lane as if it were an animal off to pasture.

SARTEANO

Sarteano

A small town in southern Tuscany, Sarteano is another of those with rings of roads and lanes around the citadel and only limited means of access from one level to the next. We entered the old town by a large brick gate to a small piazza with the expected memorials to the heroes of Italian unity and found ourselves wandering with many changes of direction up towards the tower that from a distance looked so impressive. Named Saracen tower, but with not the slightest look of eastern or Muslim origin, rather with late medieval machicolations round a solid square-based tower, it was the ultimate goal of our wanderings up the town. A goal not to be achieved: clearly the land at the top around it is in private ownership and however high we went, we never got more than the slightest glimpse of the tower through the trees. In fact the only time we saw it properly was on the way out of the modern town, northwards, when looking back over the vineyards we saw it standing proudly on the hill, having repelled invasion attempts. Our main impression of Sarteano itself is of the restored houses on various high levels, with balcony gardens, allowing more space for a pleasant modern life than usual in these walled centres.

Sarteano had little in the way of art or architecture to show us. Inside the walls the only place we visited was the church of S. Martino, heavy and dark, with a beautiful Beccafumi painting. The church of S. Francesco, outside the main gate as so often in the case of the friary buildings, was in contrast light, airy, almost barn-like. Remnants of unidentified fresco fragments could be seen in different parts of this brick church. There was also a plaque, put up in 1905, to Alberto di Sarteano, a member of the local Berdini family who had died many years before the plaque in 1385. He provided us with an interesting link to the gaunt face that was beginning to haunt us, from picture after picture, of Saint Bernardino of Siena, one of the firebrands of the early Franciscans. Albert was here identified as a close friend of the saint.

MONTEPULCIANO

Montepulciano

Unusually, we motored up to almost the highest point of this town, parking just below the Fortressa in front of S. Maria dei Servi, a small and closed baroque church. The view, one of many to be gained from the town, was across the valley to the southern Tuscan hills, quite different from Umbria, wider and drier expanses, more long ridges and less pimples, certainly less trees mostly small formations of cypresses climbing up a slope, all interspersed with "bad lands", cratered and canyoned depressions of dry mud colour. We had come from the green of Umbria to the tan of Tuscany, vividly different even in winter.

A unexciting walk down the gentle slope to the Piazza Grande opened on to a truly theatrical setting. No building to the far right and a broken-down duomo facade behind us, three fine palazzi and a fountain provided a

Renaissance setting. Strictly the Palazzo Comunale to the left originated in the thirteenth century; this building had been added to and given a tower to make it echo the Florentine Palazzo Vecchio, signifying the political dominance of Florence here The other two palazzi, designed by Sangallo, were pure Renaissance, uniform and regular in appearance. This architect contributed so much to Montepulciano and his special contribution would be our treat later in the day. The town seems as though it has stood still since the sixteenth or seventeenth century.

Montepulciano

The duomo facade looks even more ruinous in reality that we expected, none of the facing stone having ever been provided. Could there possibly be anything behind that jumble of old stone and brick worth looking at? Once inside, only one object drew immediate attention. It was as dramatic and as much in its right place anything we had seen; the altarpiece by the late medieval Sienese artist, Taddeo di Bartoli, burning and glistening in the dark spacious cathedral. Such Sienese triptychs, polyptychs and the like are to be seen, and admired, in art galleries and museums throughout Italy, and through the world. But here was one, and one of the most beautiful, complete and in its right place above the altar in this place of worship. It is a triptych dedicated to Our Lady, with three main scenes, three upper cameos, four pillars of saints standing one above the other and a set of miniature predella scenes along the lower stage. Gold was the dominant colour in which figures were placed and red the most common for the robes. Well-lit, it glows above the altar.

There were other treasures in the cathedral, small items of beauty in a well-kept if plain place of worship. Eye-catching was a small Madonna and Child of Sano di Pietro, from a slightly later date than the triptych, set on a pillar, with a wide-eyed and almost doleful look on both Mother and Child. Almost hidden away in a corner was a carved white altar attributed to Andrea della Robbia sited in a chapel above a baptismal font. In a number of places, including either side of the high altar were marble statues, the work of Michelozzo, six of them, that had at one time been part of the now broken-up monument to a papal secretary, Bartolomeo Aragazzi. All these items complemented the triptych and occupied our attention until it was time to return back and appreciate again the work of Taddeo di Bartolo.

The walk through the town to the Porta al Prato and back gave an overall impression of massive Renaissance palazzi, impressive and heavy, usually not in very good condition and including one extraordinary oddity; on occasion the whole lowest section was almost entirely made up of Etruscan funerary stones. The church of Sant'Agostino, designed by Michelozzi, contained Sienese pictures and a haunting crucifix attributed to Donatello. Inevitably the church with the "fabulous Signorelli" painting was closed, one of the few drawbacks of seeing such places out of season.

Montepulciano, San Biagio

The town still had one special place to offer the art enthusiast, or any lover of beauty for that matter. A drive off the fortress area and a short route down an avenue of cypress trees led to the pilgrimage church of San Biagio. The comparison with the parallel church in Todi, Santa Maria della Consolasione, was all in favour of this at Montepulciano, whether the colour of the stone, the peaceful isolation of its site or even more the harmony of the inside. Here, no excessive baroque decoration marred the dignity of the architecture. To complete the scene, a loggia designed by the same architect, Antonio di Sangallo, stood just to the side of the platform on which San Biagio was placed. The two buildings together evoked a Renaissance "package" of canons living in the loggia, serving the pilgrimage temple, even if some of its pilgrims on this winter day were a few centuries late.

Montepulciano barrels

Montepulciano is, of course, especially known for its wine and although we were not making any study of this and were no experts, we were able to visit one cantina just outside the town, with a good view over towards the town. This provided us with a good example of the great barrels and boxes of bottles framed by nearby vineyards and in the middle distance the historic town on its hill, the marriage of two great joys for so many visitors.

PIENZA

Coming to Pienza from the north through almost arid land and a minimal suburb brings us to the Murello Gate, with a beautiful frescoed city scene with angels sheltered under the upper arch: even if it has been restored by a modern local painter, it epitomizes the character of the place, self-contained, a single foundation of one man's vision and small enough to be contained in one's mind's grasp. The alternative route to Pienza we took another time was more attractive as an approach, from the south with the small city always in view on the hill above the Orcia valley. In this case arrival is at a small car park below the cathedral and balcony walls, allowing just a short walk through a town gate up to the main piazza.

Pienza, church tower

In a sense all that is important faces onto this Piazza Pio Due, which particularly on a weekend morning hosts the gathering and meeting, the intermixing of the inhabitants only to become totally empty during the ensuing siesta. Aeneo Silvio Piccolomini, now Pope Pius II, may have been simply promoting himself in creating his own Pienza out of Corsignano, but this does not affect

209

the end result which achieves a harmony rarely found in the towns of southern Tuscany and Umbria, retained even in the rebuild of the bombed quarter, restored since the Second World War. The Pope set the tone to the ensemble with the cathedral, a very simple balanced Renaissance design in white travertine, contrasting with the sandstone or brick almost exclusively used alsewhere. In comparison, the Palazzo Piccolomini, the family home for centuries after, is almost a fortress. Pius II tried to insist that his cardinals and their families build further palazzi with the result that the designs and building materials around the Piazza differ according to the various family origins. The loggia which unusually fronts the Town Hall plays a secondary role in the scene despite its tall tower scarred by marks of wartime bullets and shells. An "extra" part is taken by the Pozzo de' cani, a well-head in Travertine stone like that of the the duomo. An attendant in other dress is the brick next-door neighbour of the Palazzo Ammanati. This characterization seems appropriate because the Piazza is surely a stage set whose widest side is filled by the cathedral.

Pienza

Inside, the cathedral is totally unexpected and different, Gothic not Renaissance, German gothic rather than French. The mood is one of lightness, a brilliance particularly if the sun is shining directly in, but accompanied by a sense of foreboding as soon as one realises that the whole altar end of the cathedral could collapse down the cliff side: great ominous cracks are there and even if we are informed that steps have been taken to prevent such a disaster, no-one can be certain and the danger is still very real. It almost seems a judgment on Pius II, whose arms and insignia are everywhere, on wall, floor and vault. Judiciously placed round the apse are five magnificent alterpieces in the Sienese style, none of them the work of the greatest names of the art world but each a treasure of figures set in a gold surround, each the centre of its own chapel. In our haphazard inhalation of the spirit of the art, these provided early and favourable reaction to the Sienese artists of whom two of the most active around here seem to have been Sano di Pietro and Matteo di Giovanni.

Pienza Palazzo

The other building here we visited was the Piccolomini palace; again Pius II never seemed far away and it has been the home of the family here right into the second half of the twentieth century. Inside is a courtyard, a square well open to the sky, through whose colonnades a small car could, and did, drive in and park; the present day custodian has such a privilege. Once the internal walls of this were painted trompe l'oeil but most of this has now faded, though the courtyard still retains an air of dignified nobility. One facade of the palazzo, like the cathedral, faces down the cliff, where a formal Italian garden sits precariously on the edge, for the moment securely held up by a retaining wall. This facade is not easy to view, partly because the garden was out of bounds, but glimpses can be gained from the path around the walls outside to reveal three magnificent loggias above each other. One could well imagine listlessly lingering out long summer days looking out on the view. And what a view, one which can now more easily be seen from the terrace path reached to the left of the cathedral from the piazza and providing a perfect balcony on which to pause. Monte Amiata presides over long rolling plains, with occasional dwelling or trees on the ridges but mostly a great emptiness. Around the rim of the view are smaller distant summits, some with a tower or fortified village, a deep grey-blue in the south. The walk round this wall, with plenty of stops to look at the view, was a wonderfully lazy counterpart to the climbs we were so often working at in Umbrian towns.

We were not in Pienza at the right time to visit the small museum and when we were, later, we somehow found wandering round the small city a more attractive prospect. Having heard that a film of Romeo and Juliet had been made here some years ago, we were now brought right up to date by the posters proudly proclaiming the winning of Oscars by the "English Patient" whose Italian elements belonged to Pienza. We looked forward to seeing our places on film.

We completed our visit with two completely different remnants from the time before Pius II created his time capsule of the early Renaissance. First, the church of St. Francis, close by the Piazza, the only medieval remnant inside the town, could not have been more different from the cathedral. Dark instead of light, musty rather than clean, a heavy hall of a church with little of special interest except for a "Virgin of Mercy" attributed to Signorelli, with the familiar figures of Saints Sebastian and Bernardino. The cloisters belonging to the church are now part of a hotel-restaurant and usually out of view, but we had a glimpse of the restored arcades of what could be a lovely place to stay.

Pieve Corsignano

The second place of this older era involved us in a gentle walk from the main gateway to the north, part way down the hillside. The parish church of St. Vitus, the old church of Corsignano, predecessor of Pienza, just has a farmhouse as a companion, and was shut. We failed to get in despite the efforts of a friendly Italian who was visiting the farm house in his three-wheeled truck and who was at first sure that they would have a key. It probably did not matter because we still saw the special Romanesque facade with unexpected female caryatid sculptures on the window above the door. The tower, round, buttressed by pilasters, with very simple window openings near the top, is unrestored and reminds us of the circular Norman towers of Norfolk. Apparently, Eneo Silvio Piccolomini was baptised in the font inside but to see it was unnecessary; we could still savour the simple old remnant of the "Den of thieves", as it was called, which he had transformed into his Pienza, even if he had not lived to see it finished into the great monument he planned.

Pienza

SPEDALETTO

Just south of Pienza was a haunting spot for a momentary stop: in medieval times it was just that, a safe haven for travellers overnight when on the pilgrimage road to Rome. It makes its appearance beside the road as a crenellated wall with twin towers, penetrated by an arch, like one of the plywood castles made for toy soldiers. The impression was somewhat dissipated by large agricultural industrial lorries turning off at the same spot and down a lane. Once inside the gateway, two completely different worlds appeared. To the left was a chapel-like building, locked by a modern door, and then a series of well-modernised appartments still perfectly in keeping with the stonework of the castle and one could imagine them to be twentieth century equivalents of their medieval predecessors. To the right, under one great tower, all was dereliction, completed by the appearance of what could honestly only be described as a hag straight out of the pages of Sir Walter Scott's "Abbot". Almost incomprehensibly she suggested we look into an inner courtyard, with its broken windows and doors, old stone ramp and cobbles among the weeds. It was not inviting for a long look.

Spedaletto

When we continued our inspection of Spedaletto by going round to the south side of the building, a muddled facade with two towers presented an extraordinary mixture of the broken-down and the completely uninhabitable, despite what must be actual signs of some habitation. Hens poked out of certain apertures, bits of washing hung on others, stacks of wood here, broken panes and slates there, the whole assembly of a medieval town slum in the middle of the countryside, up to the height of four or five storeys, stone patched with brick, all under the crenellations and broken machicolations of the medieval guardian of the traveller pilgrims.

MONTICCHIELLO

Monticchiello

Beyond Spedaletto to the south east of Pienza, we climbed the road up to Monticchiello and parked on a viewpoint just outside the fortified village. The contrast was considerable although here again we were visiting a medieval site, for it was fully inhabited and well-kept. The old wall was very nearly complete, the upper part of the village now enclosed rough land and allotments where there were originally dwellings. Maybe this slight under-population could be a reminder of the disaster time when nearly the whole population were killed after a siege, or so goes the story. At the very top was a mini-version of a Rocca, now just a tower which someone had repaired with patches of concrete but which now was cracking again and falling back to ruin. The village was tidy, sloping streets, little piazzas with hints in the architecture of the buildings of grander ages and a large parish church entered up a wide set of steps.

Inside there should have been a painting by Pietro Lorenzetti, but it was away for restoration. Instead, what we found, for the church was open, was a beautifully maintained sanctuary with large numbers of frescoes of various dates by more or less unknown painters: altogether it was a good assemblage. On the left of the main altar was a particular fresco which dominated the church, a giant S. Cristoforo, so often the largest of saints in representation and here almost the height of the building, appropriate since the church was dedicated to saints Leonardo and Cristoforo. On the right of the altar was the remnant of a similar fresco but too damaged for any certain identification. Another much smaller fresco was a very attractive one belonging to the school of Simone Martini. Unusually, the building was very well lit, especially by a fine if restored rose window in the west wall. Altogether a pleasing if undistinguished church, despite the absence of Lorenzetti. The question of if or when the picture would be returned from restoration in Siena reminded us of the worry and complaint often voiced in Pienza where they firmly believed that their treasures were either being leached away by the provincial capital or were being denied legitimate financial help to maintain them.

S. ANNA IN CAMPRENA

This was a place where our persistance was finally rewarded. Twice we had made our way here out of Pienza hoping to find it open but were frustrated not just by very limited opening times, weekends only, but that even these times were not adhered to. The third time, there were a large number of cars here just before the appointed time and a crowd assembled outside from various countries, mainly Italians, French and Americans. Obviously "The English Patient" had caused this pilgrimage but even now the doors were not opened at the stated time and some impatient young Italians sped away in their Ferrari. When the custodian did arrive, there was a surge to the door and a mad rush to the appropriate rooms belonging to the film scenes. Apart from one French group and two other couples, the crowd of sixty or seventy people zoomed in, rushed ahead to their appointed places and within less than a quarter of an hour had almost totally disappeared. They had done their pilgrimage and were on their way in cars leaving just few people to wander freely and in peace.

S. Anna

The old convent has been partly restored, especially the church and the refectory. Everywhere else, in the cloisters, outside the monastic buildings, in the gardens and throughout the rest there is clear evidence of major restoration work going on, presumably aided by the finance from its use by the film producers. The kitchen, various store rooms and bedroom cubicles were on view for film devotees: even rumpled bed linen remained on the cot-like beds. The church is a simple hall building with sparse furnishings and has the sad air of a deserted place of worship. For us the particular reason for visiting S. Anna was the refectory with Sodoma frescoes on the walls at either end, six in all although only four of them can easily be identified. The Pieta over the entrance door was to our mind especially fine although the other two at that end, a Madonna and Child and St. Benedict, were well restored and impressive. The Feeding of the Multitude by Jesus at the other end, very appropriate here in the refectory, was a very full composition while Sodoma's love of adding animals into his work was well in evidence. Despite the crowds we had found at the beginning of our visit we were here able to peruse the frescoes at our leisure and with hardly anyone else present.

The whole site of the convent, especially as the crowds melted, was a beautiful one on a hill surrounded by mixed trees and looking out over the Sienese bad-lands towards the village of Petroio and others. It seemed a sort of annex to Monte Oliveto Maggiore, although no actual connection, being for a different sex of religious; hopefully it will be restored as a cultural site thanks to "The English Patient". Much later our viewing of the film brought back happy memories.

PETROIO

Petroio

In the heart of the terracotta-making area, we found the village of Petroio and dared the car up the narrow streets, as it seemed, round and round the hill to a little piazza next to the parish church of S. Andrea. There was just room to park the car and we were welcomed here by a little Italian, very friendly and as he saw the GB sticker, quick to tell us he had spent two years in England as a prisoner of war from Tunisia. The church of S. Andrea was open, was beautifully kept and maintained; later we noticed the priest going in to check it. We did not expect to find any special art and so were pleasantly surprised to find cared-for frescoes at the east end centred on a Crucifixion with various saints by a relatively unknown but clearly very competent Sienese artist, Andrea di Niccolo, dating from end of the fifteenth century. Underneath, the fresco continued with a depiction of Christ rising from the tomb, the same iconography as that used by Perugino as we saw in the National Gallery of Perugia. This was further proof if any was needed of our assertion that almost anywhere in this area one may find beautiful pictures, and still in situ.

We continued to walk round the village, at whose summit was a tall stone tower, the remains of a castle, which dominated the silhouette of the village from a distance. The various views from the streets were magnificent even if interrupted by the brick chimney of a terracotta works actually in the village. One could be in no doubt of the life-blood of this region. Our visit was completed by a drive down a forty or more degree slope, round a right-angle bend, thankfully one-way.

CENNANO

After Petroio, we did not stop in Castelmuzzio itself but just beyond made our way up a lane towards a building overlooked by a great forbidding builder's crane. Here was the Pieve di S. Stefano at the hamlet of Cennano, one of the very oldest churches in southern Tuscany. Restoration work was clearly in progress, they had just about completed the re-roofing and the lunch-time break stopped all present activity. The church looks quite small from outside and is, at least in part, from earlier than the eleventh century. It sported primitive but clear carvings over the doorways, west and south, some of which were hardly Christian or to be expected in a church, including one which was clearly a feminine fertility symbol leaving nothing to the imagination.

An advantage of the work actually being done was that the church was open, the builders relaxing nearby kicking a ball around. It appeared amazingly large inside, high with impressive pillars and was set out for use as a concert hall. In fact, a program from six months ago was still on one of the chairs. This site was a fascinating contrast to the church visited in Petroio; almost side-by-side in Tuscan hills, the early Renaissance place of worship well cared-for preserved in an old fortified village, and the Carolingian church almost alone beside a small vineyard, retained and being restored for cultural uses only.

MONTE OLIVETTO MAGGIORE

Arrival at the monastery at lunchtime allowed us to imbibe both the grounds and their setting on the hillside before going into the buildings themselves. The whole site is extraordinary, on a limb stuck out over riven valleys, a promontory which is not only the result of past erosion but the object of present eroding forces whose destructive power is very real. Many of the roads in the area are continually being repaired after erosion damage while that onto the promontory is a feat of engineering and provides spectacular and dramatic views down the grey clay scarps. The surrounds of the abbey seem held together by great trees, cypress, pine and others, forming a guarded entry drive but also protecting the tranquility of the place. The quasi-fortification of the old monastery is borne out by the gatehouse, massive in brick with a drawbridge, but at the same time decorated with a beautiful Della Robbia glazed terracotta of the Virgin in glistening colour clearly advertising the religious nature of the buildings. The parallel terracotta on the inside of the gatehouse has an eastern look about the seated figure, almost as if it were Chinese. From the gatehouse, especially as we were almost the only visitors there, the way down to the monastery was silent in the trees which hid the abbey until the very last moment. In between we passed one of the small Renaissance chapels which was in process of being restored, together with a vast walled "reservoir".

Monte Olivetto church

We were allowed into the brick-built monastery at 3.15 p.m., and according to notices one of the monastery services was at 3.30 p.m. Wondering whether this would affect our visit to the church, we went there first. The service was actually held somewhere below, down some steps from the transept. As we stood in the church the sense of monastery came alive as white-robed monks came through and down the stairs, some on their own, one lighting candles in church on his way, two separately with young men in mufti, groups of two or three, some rushing, others taking their time, of all ages from twenty year-olds to one, probably eighty or more, shuffling and with a plaster on his forehead. At the end came a noticeably impressive figure, dressed the same way but probably the abbot or prior. We were very much aware of the active monastery adding pertinence to the beauty of the building and particularly of the art which was the primary reason for our visit. Throughout this visit monks passed us, mostly taking no apparent notice at all, some giving us friendly looks when appropriate; one wondered how far visitors like us, especially at the height of the season instead of in February, were a terrible imposition into their contemplative life.

The church is beautiful, refurbished much later than the medieval period but retaining a medieval atmosphere despite the Baroque decoration, the fine Renaissance choir stalls and great lectern. The main treasure of the monastery is to be found in the adjacent cloister, where the frescoed life of Saint Benedict covers all four inside walls in a magnificent set of pictures, nine by Signorelli, the other twenty-seven by Il Sodoma. They are well-known in the art history of Renaissance frescoes, but the special privilege, here on a weekday afternoon in February, is to be able to take one's time wandering through the cloister, sitting between the arches which led into the garth, looking at each picture in turn knowing that the white-robed monks of St. Benedict's story may at any moment be reflected in a living one passing by. Many of the little details, small figures in the background, countryside scenes with feathery trees, animals from Il Sodoma's managerie complement the main stories and demand a quiet gaze, not just a glance.

Monte Olivetto

One disadvantage of this time of year was that other parts of the monastery, such as the refectory or library, were not available for viewing; we therefore moved on eventually to the abbey shop, selling products and cards in one of the outbuildings. On a second visit, showing those staying with us round our "gem", we were able to go up the staircase out of the cloister and look into the refectory, but there was some restoration work being done: we could just see the potential of these further frescoes. Outside again we could view the vast extent of the monastery, corridors and cloisters, dominated by the great brick tower over the church. Truly a magical place made the more so by the presence of the benign white-robed monks, quietly smiling. Surely the founder from Siena would approve of our pilgrimage to this wonderful place.

S. QUIRICO D'ORCIA

S. Quirico

Our visit to S. Quirico was, we knew, going to be a very limited one at the end of the afternoon. In fact there was something of a fiesta going on in the small town so that we would not have been able to see the sights in the centre, but we were able to park below the brick town wall and go into the Collegiata. The outside of this church is on the grand scale with superb Romanesque carvings over and around the two main doors, one dating to the eleventh century, the other a little later. The piazza around was shared between the Collegiata and a great family palazzo, crumbling and decayed, in much need of expensive restoration, which must once have presented a fine Renaissance facade to balance the Romanesque. Maybe it will once again look at its best some day. Inside the church the hoped-for triptych by Sano di Pietro was there and beautiful. The whole church was full of Romanesque and later details, paintings and carvings: it was with some regret that we had only a fleeting visit to this beautiful place.

BAGNO VIGNONI

Bagno Vignoni

227

By the valley of the Orcia river this place is really nothing but two or three hotels, half a dozen houses and what could be described as a piazza in water at its centre. The hot spring rises rowards one end of the pool, bubbling all the time into greenish water steaming into the cooler air and all surrounded by low-key Renaissance architecture which owes its existence to the patronage of the Medici. Bathing is no longer allowed, so either people stroll around the pool or repair to one of the hotels which has channelled a supply of the water into its own pool. In the stone wall surrounds of the pool a number of small fig trees have found a foothold and were just bursting into leaf. The surplus water from this great bath flows down a channel mostly covered over by stone to the hillside at the south of the hamlet. Here is a rock face dripping down to the Orcia river and the warm sulphurous water is allowed to ooze out of the channel on to the rock and to find its own way, or ways, down the rock to which it gives strange colours and textures. This spot as well as giving views on this strange waterfall trickle is a vantage point for seeing the river below, the old bridge across it and the castellated villages of Castiglione and Rocca above and beyond. To the east stretch the wide plains of the upper river while to the west the hills crowd in to make a mini-gorge.

CASTIGLIONE D'ORCIA

Castiglione d'Orcia

Of the two routes up to Castiglione we chose the longer one instead of that straight up under Rocca, which may be more dramatic, but the longer prolongs the gradually increasing anticipation. This meant that we arrived in one of the two main squares from which we could walk up and round the remains of the ancient castle. The second piazza celebrates the birthplace of the Sienese artist Lorenzo di Pietro, called Il Vecchietta, whose work was much in evidence as we found in the Baptistry at Siena. The old cobbled irregular piazza with medieval houses clustered to it gave us an idea of the home and origin of one of these typical Sienese artists, but we wondered, how it all must have changed. When we arrived in the parish church of Saints Stefano and Degna, there was just one small Madonna and Child by Lorenzetti instead of the group of paintings expected. A disappointment in a pleasant medieval church well cared-for by among others a family, parents and young children, who were attending to things here on Saturday. Later, we found one major painting missing from here now in the Pinacoteca at Siena, one of at least three important pictures purloined from this area. Even more attractive as a building is the other church of the village, that of S. Maria Maddalena on the outskirts dating from about the eleventh century. It has some old fresco fragments and exudes a wonderful air of the ancient appealing to our love of the Romanesque. We were pleasantly surprised to find the churches open in this village even in the middle of the day.

ROCCA D'ORCIA

Rocca d'Orcia

Identified on notices as a Borgo, this is a far more dramatic place with the huge donjon dominating both its own hamlet and the village of Castiglione. We walked into it at the bottom of the direct road up to Castiglione through a charming small gateway and following the winding road up past well-restored houses and a small piazza, a set of steps, another piazza; it was almost like a stage-set village on a mini-scale clinging to the hillside. Over halfway up we came to the church of S. Simeone outside which sat an old peasant woman. She was bursting with enthusiasm to show us round and to point out to us all the treasures she so obviously revered. Once again the best known painting, a Madonna by Giovanni di Paolo, was missing and we later found it in Siena but there was still much to see even if not "great art". In a sense pictures and statues such as we found here are a village art that in any other part of the world would get important notices; we are glad to find that they were treasured by such a wonderful old peasant lady who acted as host for her village. This is the real art of the churches, of the people.

Though it was open. we did not go into the castle but walked all around the base on a steep path through the flowers; this gave us a good chance to appreciate the position of almost impregnable strength high above the plain. We could easily be transported back in time: even the gardeners in the plots above and around the houses of the Borgo seemed to be doing much the same things as they would have done in medieval times even if now with better tools and materials.

MONTALCINO

Montalcino

Just occasionally the well-known sites we visited failed to live up to expectation: Montalcino on a Sunday morning was one and probably would have been on any other day. The initial problem was that without a good map of the town we found ourselves going backwards and forwards and getting nowhere; I do not think it was entirely our fault. Deadends were a feature of the place, there was no clear single street through, neither was the main piazza one at all but rather a disjointed widened road in two parts. Here was a tall but not very distinguished Palazzo Civico. The cathedral building was open but invited little interest. The Museum of Art into which two collections seem now to have been joined, was firmly closed for restoration and with no indication of any future opening. The Romanesque church of S. Agostino with fourteenth century frescoes was firmly closed, for restoration. The only places open seemed to be for selling the expensive wine, for the pursuit of Brunello.

Montalcino rocca

Then we came back to the Rocca. In many towns the Rocca was either of little interest except for views or was in private ownership, but in this case the five-sided extensive curtain walls of the fourteenth century fortress were well worth the visit for themselves while within one tower was the Enoteca, the destination of most visitors. Here we could well believe the story of the last independent government of Siena trying to defy the might of Medicean Florence, the successful rebuttal of armies. On the corner of the prow of the fortress, above where we had parked, was a massive reproduction of the Medici coat of arms: in the end they had made their presence surely felt. We were left with a very mixed taste from Montalcino, situated as it is between the open folds of southern Tuscany and the edge of the Maremma wooded hills. But it was the starting point of two superb abbey visits.

SANT'ANTIMO

Sant' Antimo

233

Sunday afternoon in March at Sant'Antimo was an Italian family day out. There were two coach loads and the contents of twenty or more cars, nearly all Italian, to fit into one church and the immediately surrounding 'park' of no more than two hundred metres each way. This sounds horrific for a trip to an ancient abbey known to be sited in a peaceful Tuscan valley. In reality our visit was very enjoyable and the behaviour of the visitors in no way spoiled it for us, rather they enhanced it. We had our lone trips to isolated places on other occasions and we could well imagine Sant'Antimo alone, isolated, silent; but possibly a bit too gaunt and haunting.

The church is all that remains of the old abbey; the last bits of old monastic building incorporated into modern barns are insignificant. Apparently now in good repair, the church is Romanesque with impressive apses and friezes of carving outside, while magnificent rows of pillars in both nave and around the ambulatory give shape to the inside. The golden colour of the stone enriched by a significant amount of a type of marbled alabaster gives texture to the simple architecture and the typically Romanesque sculpturing on the capitals. The hanging crucifix of painted wood in what is described as Catalan style above the altar is one of the most powerfully expressive we have seen. There are early frescoes on sections of walling expecially at the east end and quite a large fresco of St. Christopher on one of the pillars. These must be just the remnants of colouring belonging to the old church, but to our taste the Romanesque architecture needed no more than these fragments.

Sant' Antimo

There were other features not so immediately obvious which we found in time. The tiny crypt entered at the side of the chancel has a primitive fresco of Christ rising out of a stone box-like tomb, an early example of imagery developed so much by the later artists. After this we were lucky that the caretaker or custodian decided to let a group of visitors see the sacristy, normally locked up, where the few remaining monks kept their robes and service books: we tagged on to the group. The interest here was in the unexpected frescoes around the room illustrating the Life of St. Benedict, painted in black and white, rather primitively with amusing animals details including a rat looking up at the saint. One imagined the monks preparing for the early morning service being given a twinkle of amusement before going on to their Gregorian chant.

The countryside around the abbey showed possibilities of walks off in a number of directions. The odd Italian couple this Sunday would be wandering off to find the wild asparagus hidden iin the undergrowth whilst others were playing with a Frisbee or were listening to a lecture on the architectural details with great intensity. The whole scene was one of a very human enjoyment of the holy site enriching many lives. On a last walk round we noticed how just to the south of the main apses, a darker apse, now the outside of the sacristy, was much older-looking than the rest of the building and presumably the remnant of the earlier abbey church, probably founded by or at the time of Charlemagne. We could at least begin to imagine periods of history peopled by monks more or less isolated here and we were just thankful that last century's shutting down of monasteries had not completely destroyed such places as Sant'Antimo.

Sant' Antimo

SAN GALGANO

We arrived at San Galgano on our way out of the area, to visit a second great monastery, now ruined; in addition we found unexpectedly a hermitage chapel of great beauty as well. The abbey buildings have all been well restored as can be clearly seen by comparison with photographs taken in the early part of the nineteenth century. In particular, the Gothic church, one of the earliest of its type in Italy and deriving directly from France, is now complete architecturally except for the roof: many of the arches in the aisles and the upper sections of the clerestory have been reconstructed to give what might be called "tidiness" to the ruin. Apart from the west door, where there is a renaissance facade, the sculpture is very simple since it was obeying the tenets of the Cistercian Order; its beauty is dependent on the proportions of the arches and windows, including what must have been a superb eastern rose window above two sets of lancets. The cloister garth is empty except for two re-erected arches, but the old chapter house and cellars can ben seen in their stark Gothic simplicity owing their survival as part of the farm buildings on site after the removal of the monks. The whole complex is situated comfortably on a flat river plain, with hills and forest in the distance; immediately to the north is a wooded hill standing guard over the abbey, approachable either by a roundabout route by road following the inevitable rows of cypresses, or more immediately by a footpath.

inside San Galgano church

On this hill the Hermitage chapel is in complete contrast, in origin clearly older than the abbey. It is fully roofed, a small unique temple. Essentially a rotunda with small additions, it is surmounted by a very solid-looking cupola-type vault. Both the inside of this and the lower walling of the outside are characterised by alternating dark and light bands of stonework and terracotta. There is a small later entrance with an archway again in alternating red and white stone. The most significant addition to the rotunda is a chapel with faded but important frescoes by Lorenzetti or a close follower decorating the upper wall with scenes Cistercian abbey below. We found it a little difficult to be sure whether or not to believe fully the account of Galgano's renunciation of his knightly fighting life as dramatically shown and annotated for us in the centre of the rotunda where the hilt of a sword sticks out of a great lump of stone where he had dug it in at his conversion. It would be nice to accept this reversal of the King Arthur story where the hero buries his weapon in the rock for ever. Whether or not we do believe, here in southern Tuscany we came to the end of our pilgrimage for the moment and had found in these two buildings a summary of much that we had seen over the previous three months.

San Galgano

www.summersdale.com